Walking with the Lord

Walking with the LORD

The relevance of First John to the contemporary Christian life

Malcolm Tolbert

BROADMAN PRESS
Nashville, Tennessee

This Broadman Press book is not the official statement of the Southern Baptist Convention. The opinions expressed are those of the author, neither necessarily in agreement with nor in conflict with those of the publisher. The intent of this book is to aid in the Christian study of the Bible, and it should be read in the light of that purpose and of biblical truth.

Dewey Decimal Classification Number: 227.34
Library of Congress Catalog Card Number: 76–117299
Printed in the United States of America

21.5My70KSP

Preface

You will recognize immediately that this is not intended to be "a critical exegetical commentary." I do not mean that I have ignored the work of biblical scholars. Their contribution provides the background of this volume. But I have purposely avoided the technical aspects of exegesis except where I felt that exegesis was absolutely necessary to bring out the meaning of the text for our time.

I do not deal specifically with the introductory questions of date, authorship, place of writing, etc. Go to a good commentary (like the one by C. H. Dodd in the Moffatt series) if you wish to discover for yourself more about the historical background of 1 John. You will learn that the question of authorship is an extremely complex and difficult one. Since it is not my purpose to address myself to the problems involved in defending a position, I will refer to the person who composed 1 John as "the writer" or "the author."

I wrote the following pages to present, at least in a limited way, what 1 John has said to me, and what I think it says to my brothers and sisters who are trying to follow Jesus Christ in the twentieth century. Much of it comes out of my experiences as I have tried to teach in churches and conferences across several years. I am aware of the limitations and weaknesses of my work. It was done amid pressures of teaching, preaching, and other writings—not to mention the usual family responsibilities and personal involvements that most of us have. But if we wait for leisure in which to write, the majority of us will never do much with it. Therefore I hope that what I have written will be helpful to a few people to whom I cannot otherwise speak.

The text of 1 John to which I refer in the commentary is the Revised Standard Version. All citations from other biblical books are also taken from this version. My own study is done with the Greek text.

In conclusion, I wish to dedicate my work to my mother and father, Katie Lee and Douglas Tolbert. They reared their children in most difficult times of severe economic depression. From them I learned what self-sacrificing love means, for they denied themselves totally in order to feed, clothe, and educate their children. My interpretation of the meaning of love in 1 John is influenced in no small measure by the example of their lives.

MALCOLM TOLBERT

Contents

1

Today's Questions in a 1900-Year-Old Book

In popular music there is a recurring, poignant theme. What the world needs, we are reminded constantly, is love, more love. There has been far too much hate and hostility. In a day when humanity is threatened with extinction by nuclear weapons, when people are forced to live close together in crowded cities, and when the world has been transformed into a very small community by the speed of modern communications, we can no longer afford the luxury of hate, prejudice, and selfishness if we are to survive. It is becoming increasingly clear, especially to the young, that we have no future at all if hate does not give way to love.

The Theological Question

Too much hate; too little love. This is also a dominant note in 1 John. There has never been a time when the message of this little book was more contemporary than it is now, nineteen hundred years after it was written. In its brief compass it touches on a number of vital questions that are still extremely significant for the Christian's life. Among these are three central issues that stand at the very heart of the church's faith and life in our times.

Who is Jesus Christ? That is the central question that 1

John attempts to answer. Now this is also the crucial, all
important question for the Christian faith today. We spend
a great deal of time arguing about things that do not really
matter, or which at most are only on the periphery of the
church's life. But we are talking here about something that
stands at the very center.

The New Testament affirms that Jesus was a man—a real
flesh-and-blood human being. Indeed, the earliest followers
of Jesus knew him first as a man. He was their Rabbi, their
teacher. They lived with him. They knew that he perspired
as they did under the heat of Palestine's sun. They had seen
him when he was weary and knew that he needed rest. They
had seen him eat to satisfy hunger, drink to slake thirst.
They had been with him in times of mental and spiritual
anguish, witnessing both the flash of his anger and the tears
of his grief.

The humanity of Jesus was not some kind of staged act.
The temptations were real; Gethsemane was real; the cross
was real. However we may understand the experiences of
Jesus' life, we do an injustice to the New Testament if we
explain them in a way that takes them out of the realm of
the human situation. The New Testament affirmation of
Jesus' humanity arises out of the earliest experiences of the
church and constitutes the beginning of the Christian
story.

In the course of their experience another conviction took
root and grew in the lives of early Christians. They came to
believe that Jesus had been the means by which they had
come into contact with ultimate reality, that is, with God.
So decisive and final was Jesus Christ for their lives that
they began to call him Son of God. Jesus was the key to
their understanding of God and themselves, of the world

and the people in it, of history and the future. He became the point of departure for their ideas about everything in and beyond human experience.

Now these are the two polarities of the New Testament concept of Jesus. On the one hand, he was a genuine human being. His life was not an act in some kind of cosmic stage production. He suffered as a man suffers, knew human sorrow and needs, contracted human diseases, was prey to the whole gamut of human emotions. On the other hand, there was something that could not be explained by saying that Jesus was a great teacher, prophet, or religious reformer. He was the crucial revelation of God in the world, the point in history where God made known his nature, his purpose, and his will for humanity.

Most of the problems that have arisen about the identity of Jesus have come about when one of these polarities has been emphasized to the exclusion of the other.

The first tendency that emerged was the effort to deny the humanity of Jesus. This is the challenge that 1 John was written to meet. Some teachers had appeared in the churches of Asia Minor, teaching that God's Son had not come into the world as a real human being of flesh. These teachers are generally called gnostics, from the Greek work *gnosis,* which means knowledge.

The central concept of gnosticism was its dualistic view of the world. Matter was conceived to be evil; spirit, good. The genuine God who was pure spirit could have nothing at all to do with matter. Consequently, the creation of the material universe was attributed to a lesser deity.

Man's plight was defined in the light of this dualism. That which is good, namely, the spirit of man, is imprisoned in the universe of matter of which his own flesh is a part.

Enslaved in this prison of matter, man's spirit is in a stupor, unconscious of its origin, its present condition, or its destiny. Man's plight is not described as sin and rebellion against God but as ignorance.

What man needs is *gnosis* or knowledge that will enable his spirit to escape from the material universe and be re-united with God. The gnostic myth centered on a divine redeemer who descends from the realm of spirit into the universe. He comes into the world and arouses the spirit in man, teaching it who it is, whence it came, and what its destiny will be. Included in the knowledge is a revelation of the mysteries that will enable the liberated spirit to make its way out of the universe to eventual union with God. This is the kind of phenomenon that produced the ideas with which the author of 1 John comes to grips.

In keeping with these basic ideas, the false teachers had identified Christ as the heavenly redeemer. But because they considered matter to be evil, they denied that he was a human being. Some of these people taught that he only appeared to be human. Others taught that the divine Christ descended on Jesus at his baptism and departed prior to the crucifixion. First John seems to combat both these ideas at different places. Whatever may have been the doctrine of a particular group, gnostic dogma affirmed that the human Jesus was not the divine Christ. In opposition, the writer of 1 John contends for the conviction that Jesus is the Christ, the Son of God.

Although they arise from other sources, gnostic-like ideas are very prevalent in the Christian movement today. The tendency to remove Jesus from the world of reality and human experience is a constant temptation. Because of their reverence for Jesus, believers sometimes shrink from understanding the incarnation in genuinely human terms. Nevertheless, we must bear in mind that we do not honor him by making him something that he was not, thereby missing the whole meaning of his life.

Another trend goes in the direction of denying the uniqueness of Jesus. Although they generally admire Jesus the man, many people are not willing to confess that this man is crucial and ultimate for revelation and salvation. They do not believe that he was "designated Son of God by his resurrection from the dead" (Rom. 1:4).

This tendency has found radical expression in recent theological thought. One of the leading spokesmen of the "God is dead" movement interpreted the incarnation as an affirmation of the death of God. God became Jesus; when Jesus died on the cross, God died. What he meant by this was that modern man can no longer believe in a transcendent God. There is nothing beyond the human struggle of the here and now. Our only option is to concentrate totally on man in this life. If God is dead, in the sense that belief in a God who stands above and beyond the human scene is not possible any longer, then only man is left. Such is the point of view of some of our contemporaries.

The failure to accept the reality of Jesus' humanity results in a flight from the responsibility of the Christian in today's world. In this case the gospel is reduced to orthodox propositions about Jesus. As a consequence, people fail to perceive that a call to believe in Jesus is a call to follow him in this world.

On the other hand, the failure to believe that Jesus is God's son robs Christianity of its uniqueness and dynamic. If the day ever comes when there is no one in all the world for whom God's revelation in Jesus is crucial and decisive,

Christianity will have ceased to exist in any discernible form. A theology based on the idea that God is dead rings the death knell for both theology and the church. Anthropology, sociology, and psychology may still be pertinent in a world that does not believe that anything exists beyond itself; but theology would certainly be beside the point.

The Ethical Question

As we have seen, the gnostic teachers held that they were liberated by their knowledge. One aspect of their liberation was the belief that sin was powerless over their lives. Such people did not interpret this to mean necessarily that they had to live pure lives in the world. In fact, quite the opposite was often true. We hear of some gnostics who taught that their freedom from sin's power was best demonstrated by their indulgence in every possible kind of immoral act. In this way they could show their contempt for sin and their superiority to it.

In their denial of the reality of the incarnation, the teachers mentioned in 1 John had severed the Christian movement from its ethical foundations. Since they did not believe that Jesus was the Christ, they did not accept his life as the key for understanding Christian ethics. What Jesus the man did was not understood to have any relationship to the way a Christian was supposed to live in the world. They had effectively isolated belief from behavior, religion from morality.

Of course, if Jesus is not held to be the son of God, his life cannot be decisive for human conduct. He may be inspirational, admirable, a good example, but no more so than any other worthy person of history.

But when we affirm that God became a man, then this

Man becomes the decisive illustration in history of God's will for all men. We can even say that Jesus was the Man, the only Man. This is to say that he was the only person in history who was truly human. To be genuinely human involves being exactly what God intended man to be. All the rest of us have been less than what God desired. Therefore, to that extent we have all been less than human.

First John takes the position that the life of Jesus provides the moral tension under which Christians live. The goal of the Christian life is set forth in Jesus.

The whole question of moral standards and goals is a very live one among us today. We live in a transition period when the old standards have been renounced and new directions for morality have not been defined. A large number of young people especially have rejected what is commonly called the Victorian standards of their elders. They also reject the idea that any person or group of persons can decide what is right for the other fellow. Each person must decide in his own circumstances what he wants or ought to do.

One attempt to meet the challenge of this transition period is the so-called *situation ethics*. People who adopt this approach generally say that there is only one absolute principle—the principle of love. All decisions must be made on the basis of love. But since circumstances differ, they say, what love demands in one case may not be the solution in another. Therefore, there are no absolute moral standards. Adultery under some circumstances may be wrong; under others it may be right.

It seems obvious when we read 1 John that the writer did not interpret Christian morality as a set of rules either. On the other hand, neither did he make a principle, however noble, the basis of morality. Rather, his point of departure was life—the life of Jesus. The ultimate in goodness was the Man who had taught and lived what it meant to be under the rule of God completely—and then had been killed because he dared to do so.

The moral tension under which 1 John sets the Christian is provided by the life of Jesus. "Live as he lived; do what he said," the author writes. God is revealed in the life of Jesus as a father who loves his children at immeasurable cost to himself. Consequently, the life of self-giving love is set forth as the highest level of morality for his followers.

Clearly, no other person can be Jesus; he can only be himself. But if under the challenge of the life of Jesus he discovers what it means for him to live a life of self-sacrificing, self-giving love, he will have comprehended the goal of goodness for his own life.

No set of rules for conduct can be adequate for this moral pilgrimage, because it cannot take into consideration the complexities of the human situation. Life is always changing, presenting humanity with a constantly evolving political, economic, and social climate in which to live.

Christian morality must begin, therefore, with a commitment—not to a set of rules but to a Person. Any person who has willed to be a follower of Jesus Christ can be trusted to act on the light that comes to him in the difficult and doubtful situations of his own life. This does not mean that moral decisions are made in a vacuum. The honest follower of Jesus is anxious to receive light from any source that will help him to achieve his goal. Not only do we need to live with the gospels and attempt to understand what they mean for us today, but we also need the help, advice, and encouragement that come from compassionate, good people.

But in the final analysis each person must decide in every situation what his responsibility to God calls him to do. Even this decision is not made alone. We believe that God gives wisdom and understanding to earnest believers that will help them to make right decisions and choices.

Admittedly, this will not answer all the questions or clear up all the doubts. But there is no approach to morality and ethics that will do this. The Jewish Talmud is a good illustration of this fact. Developed by the rabbis across many centuries, it is a voluminous attempt to apply the law to all the concrete situations that a person might confront in life. If it were brought up to date, other volumes would have to be written. If this is the correct approach to morality, we would have to be scholars in order to be moral.

One other point may be made. People who accept the life and teachings of Jesus as the moral challenge to their own existence will never be satisfied with their weaknesses and failures. They will never condone nor excuse their sins. To the contrary, they will spend all their lives trying to be better.

Victorian morality, a set of rules governing society's moral life is a thing of the past. If you do not believe this, you have not watched TV recently.

But perhaps Christians will rise to the challenge presented by the moral chaos of our times. Perhaps they will find something better to put in its place as they seek to understand what it means to live under the tension of Jesus' life in the last half of the twentieth century.

The Problem of Relationships

Another problem arose from the gnostic teachers' denial of the incarnation. They had no basis for understanding what the Christians' relationship to other Christians should be.

They believed that they were saved by their knowledge. To be sure, this knowledge was imparted by the heavenly Redeemer, who had invaded the evil, material universe to bring it. But it was given at no cost to him or to them. They were convinced that their comprehension of it was due to their own superior spiritual capacity to receive it. This kind of approach breeds arrogance and divisiveness. Those who adopt it generally despise and reject people who do not share their particular point of view.

The gnostics evidently had contempt for the believers who held to their old ideas. According to their view, the more traditional Christians were out of touch with their times and lacked sophistication.

By contrast, the gospel proclaims that salvation is by grace, the unmerited favor of God poured out on people who otherwise have no hope. This concept is rooted in the conviction that Jesus, God's son, died to save men. Jesus' surrender of his own life is the supreme evidence to Christians that God loves them without limit or reservation. This is exactly what the gnostic teachers rejected, and it caused them to miss the essential meaning of the gospel.

Our experience of God's self-sacrificing love for us should serve as the basis of our love for others. We know God's love as completely undeserved love. Our relation to him as his children is made possible by his grace and is no reward for any personal merit that we may possess. When God's love for us becomes God's love in us, it reaches out to others who, like us, desperately need it precisely because they can never deserve it.

Furthermore, when God's love claims us, it makes us a

part of a great family of people whom he has also redeemed. If for no other reason, we should love God's other children simply because God loves them.

There are so many superficial, erroneous views about what being Christian really means. First John teaches that it involves being open and accepting toward our brothers. They come from varying social classes, varying races, and have a multitude of both lovable and unlovable characteristics. But more important than those factors that divide us is that bond which unites us. They are our brothers. We cannot deny them without denying their father. First John puts the matter just that simply—and just that painfully.

The great scandal of American Christianity has been racial and class prejudice. Our churches will never have a right relationship with God and, therefore, will always be eaten by the cancer of guilt and evil until they come to terms with this problem on a Christian basis. We need desperately to hear and heed what 1 John has to say to us in this area of our lives.

2

Being True to the Past

Much of the tension of our times is produced by the conflict between the old and the new. Many young people arbitrarily reject the past and all that is associated with it. The religion, morality, ideas, goals, and anything else belonging to other generations are thrown out the window.

On the other hand, other people, bewildered by the rapid changes and the revolutionary temper of our times, react instinctively against anything new. Even when the old is patently inadequate for a new set of circumstances, they refuse to relinquish it. These two extremes are irrevocably hostile and irreconcilable. They stand on either side of an unbridgeable chasm rather than a generation gap.

Only if we are able to discover the meaningful relationship between the present and the past are we going to be able to come to grips with our problems in a way that will help us to face the future with hope and optimism. This is especially true with the Christian faith.

The situation reflected in 1 John 1:1-4 is very similar to some aspects of our present dilemma. Certain people wanted to dissociate Christianity completely from its historical foundations. They wanted to persuade believers to accept novel, sensational, modern ideas and to discard their relationship with the past.

Of course, we cannot believe that God is a prisoner to

some past age. He is not a fact of history but a living, dynamic, contemporary power. He is active and involved in his world. For this reason Christian groups responsive to God will be forward-moving and creative.

Wherever God is, he is not back there in some idealized age of the past. He is out there—always out there, ahead of us. Fresh insights and fresh understandings of God and his purposes are still granted to persons who are really sensitive to what God is doing in the world.

At the same time, we cannot believe that God has been dormant in the past and has just now been aroused to activity. Such a God would be no God at all. Nor can we justly conclude that there was nothing authentic in the experiences of the past. Whatever God is doing today must have some relationship to what he has been doing all along. There was a *beginning* back there. Something happened that called the church into being. Christians cannot truly appreciate their relationship to God and what God would do through them until they see them in connection with what God did in that beginning. Whatever the church does in the present or future, it must be true to what happened when it all started.

What happened was that a group of people came to know a man who set their lives on a new course. Oh, yes, he was really a man. They had no doubt about that. They had *heard* him, *seen* him with their eyes, *touched* him with their hands.

But that event had a meaning which transcended the physical, objective nature of it. Jesus was also the *word of life*. Life or eternal life are important Johannine concepts. It is above all the life that God possesses and that he imparts. It is this qualitative rather than the quantitative

aspect which is most important. We often talk about the
fact that salvation involves living forever. But the mere
prolongation of existence is not in itself necessarily an attractive or exciting prospect. From the Hindu or Buddhist
point of view, personal existence is the source of human
misery. The goal of these religions is the cessation of personal existence and absorption into the All or God.

But *life* is the rich, meaningful, and full existence that
flows from God and that is impossible apart from him. Life
and love are closely associated in 1 John. To have life is to
know one's self loved by God and to love others. Possession
of such life is an exciting and rewarding experience. It
brings to an individual an awareness of who he is as a child
of God. Life is not petty, meaningless, futile, or tragic. It is
bound up with the life of God. It is a present possession, to
be experienced and lived in this world. At the same time, it
has a meaning that transcends the narrow confines of birth
and death, of space and time, and of the ebb and flow of
history.

God's life is communicated to men through Jesus Christ,
the *Word of life*. This is God's creative, life-giving word,
God's agent in bringing the universe into being. Now
through his Word God brings a new creation into being.
This new creation is the community that shares his life in a
new relationship of love. As 1 John will make abundantly
clear, to possess the life of God is for us to love one
another.

The life was made manifest is equivalent to the affirmation of John 1:14: "And the Word became flesh." God's
life of love was made incarnate in a human being. God
identified with man, became a part of the contradictions
and the conflicts of the human situation. This means that

God could not reach man as an abstraction, a word, an idea. It was necessary to become a man, to identify with human need, to know human sorrows and joys. It was only in this concrete and tangible way that man could ever know that he had not been abandoned by God to face the problems and questions of life alone. In spite of the despair and disillusion often produced by his experiences, man could look at Jesus and believe that God loved him.

It is to this event, the incarnation, that the earliest Christians gave witness. *That which we have seen and heard we proclaim also to you.* According to tradition, the author was himself a member of the earliest group of disciples. Most modern scholars, however, believe that the evidence is against the tradition. Whatever may be the case, *we* expresses his solidarity with the original witnesses. The experiences of the first followers of Jesus is a part of the total experience of the church, shared by all believers. The first Christians had verified the reality of the incarnation. This became the foundation of the church's witness in all generations. The New Testament is the perpetuation of this apostolic witness in succeeding generations. The unique function of the New Testament is best understood in this light; it is witness.

So the Christian is not an innovator. True enough, he is not just a reporter. His witness is based on his personal encounter with God through Jesus Christ. But his understanding of his own encounter is related to the genuine experience of those first Christians. In this the writer of 1 John had to surrender something to his opponents.

They were not bound by the past, so they were able to give free reign to their own imaginations. They could resort to the new and sensational, be scornful of the provincial,

backward ideas of Christians who insisted on holding to
outmoded beliefs about the Christian gospel. The attacker
always has the advantage of this kind of mobility. It is
hardly sensational to affirm one's faith in Jesus Christ and
in the redemptive significance of the gospel. No one will
make the headlines in this way.

There is a way, however, in which a genuine Christian
can be exciting and different. He may decide to follow Jesus
in the radical commitment of his life. To affirm one's faith
in words is not sensational; to live out one's faith in deeds is
indeed sensational and revolutionary in any age.

Why did the word become flesh? The answer is to create
fellowship. The Greek word *koinonia* denotes a meaningful
and rich New Testament concept. The English word *fellowship* is so watered down that it hardly does justice to its
Greek counterpart. Fellowship often signifies no more than
good-natured fun at a social gathering, or meaningless
chit-chat about inconsequential, noncontroversial subjects.

Here, however, it is used to describe the relationship of
Christians to God and to one another. In meaning it is very
close to the Pauline concept of the body of Christ. Those
who belong to Christ also belong to one another. They
share together in the life of God. In fact, this life is only
mediated to men as a shared life. There is no basis in the
New Testament for the idea that men are saved in isolation
from others. If we understand the biblical concept of the
purpose of God in its broad sweep, it is not the salvation of
individual "souls" but the creation of community.

The center of this community or fellowship is Jesus
Christ. This is true for two reasons. He has bridged the gap
between God and man. Through Jesus man is reconciled to
God. Furthermore, he has bridged the gap between man

and man, reconciling men to each other. These are two sides of the same coin. Human hostility, prejudice, hate, and greed are factors of man's alienation from God. Reconciliation with God and reconciliation with man are thus bound up together. The expression of this fact is the Christian community.

All those who acknowledge Jesus as their Lord are also my brothers. Relationship to Jesus involves relationship with his body. This is fundamental to the right understanding of the church. We have tried in our selfishness to make the church an organization from which we could exclude those who do not agree with us or with whom we do not wish to associate. In recent years, for example, churches have quite frequently voted to exclude people from their "fellowship" on the basis of race. We need to understand something very clearly. We can bring an organization into being, elect deacons, officers and teachers, and call a pastor. We can give the name "church" to this organization, but this does not in fact make it a church. If a group adopts any standards that exclude people from its fellowship that God has accepted into his, they have disqualified themselves from being a church. They have become a social club. Whether or not a person is a part of the body of Christ is not determined by the vote of a group of people who pride themselves on their rights and privileges (a thoroughly non-biblical concept). A church is brought into being by God's gracious, redeeming activity and not by the consent or vote of a group of people.

First John calls the Lord of the community *Jesus Christ,* the *Son of God.* He uses these names very deliberately. Jesus is the translation of the Greek equivalent of the Hebrew Joshua, a very popular name among Jewish people.

Names were often chosen as expressions of faith and hope. Joshua, meaning Jahweh saves, was such a name. This was the name given to Jesus when he was born, the name by which his family called him, the name by which he was known to his friends and associates.

It was the name of the man who had been crucified not long since under Pontius Pilate. It was also the name used in the gnostic circles to identify the human being. Christ is the translation of *Christos* the Greek equivalent of the Hebrew Messias, meaning the "anointed one." The Messiah was the one many Jews expected to appear as the bearer of God's judgment and salvation. In the gnostic circles, however, Christ had been used to designate the heavenly redeemer as distinct from the human Jesus.

But the affirmation of faith found in this writing is that Jesus is the Christ. The human Jesus cannot be isolated from the divine redeemer. He is also the Son of God. Unlike later generations, early Christians did not try to explain the mystery and uniqueness of this life. They simply affirmed the conviction of their own experience and faith. Many Christians today feel a real kinship for those early Christians. Also the Christological formulations, the trinitarian formulas, and other statements that seek to explain the mystery of God's entrance on the human scene in the person of Jesus Christ hardly explain it to them at all. But all believers know that God's revelation of himself in Jesus is the decisive event for their existence and the basis of their faith and hope in today's world.

The fellowship of believers with God and one another through Jesus Christ is the source of fullest *joy*. Christian joy reaches its highest point in the relationship with our brothers and sisters in Christ.

We need our brothers. Otherwise, we live out our lives in loneliness and estrangement. Without them we are twisted, warped, and made miserable by suspicion, prejudice, and narrowness. There is no joy in a life of recrimination and bitterness. This is not the soil in which it flourishes. Joy is possible only where there is love and acceptance. It is known in its fullest when we become instruments through which the reconciling grace of God can flow to break down walls, heal divisions, and bind up the wounds of broken humanity.

3

The Question of Morality

The believer and the unbeliever start from different points in their attitude toward the whole question of ethics and morality. The basis of the believer's approach to morality must necessarily be what he believes about God. The biblical stance on moral issues is grounded in the belief that God is holy, good, and righteous. The corollary in terms of human behavior is inevitable. A good God expects goodness from men. The highest worship of such a God is not in ritual and sacrifice but in a life shaped by his goodness. Because of this the prophets and Jesus denounced empty ritual and called for commitment to love, justice, and mercy.

The God of the gnostic teachers was wholly divorced from the world and the human struggle. The ethical ideas of the prophets and the earliest Christian preachers simply had no relevance to such a God, who existed as pure, impassive spirit in an exalted heaven without any connection at all with the world.

Religion and Life
1 John 1:5–7

Our writer affirms that *God is light* without any *darkness at all*. Light is a natural, universal symbol of deity. It is associated with illumination, knowledge, security, and pur-

28

ity. This term was an important part of gnostic vocabulary. The false teachers thought of light in abstract terms, probably associating it with an ethereal realm completely removed from the universe of matter.

But in 1 John light has an ethical content. The author is emphasizing the moral character of God. Later on we shall learn that he thinks primarily about love as the central and controlling force of the character of God. God is wholly good and is completely untouched by evil. This, says the writer, is what we learned *from him,* that is, from Jesus. For the Christian the highest insight into the character of God comes from Jesus. We cannot read the gospels without reaching the conclusion that Jesus believed, taught, and lived by the conviction that God *is* totally good.

From this basic conviction about God the writer draws a conclusion about believers. The profession of one's relationship with God must be attested by the character of one's life. The verb *walk* is a hebraism. It comprehends the total expression of one's life in the world as a thinking, speaking, living, acting, and interacting human being. The way one walks is the way one lives in the world. Every word spoken, every attitude formed, every relationship established, every decision made—all of this is involved.

The writer's conclusion is that there must be a vital relationship between belief and behavior. If one's belief in God does not affect all areas of his life, his profession is a *lie.*

Lie does not have exactly the meaning that we associate with it. We think of lying as a deliberate distortion of facts. However, in this case to lie is to live a deceived and deluded existence. A person thinks that he has a relationship with God when in fact, the obverse is true. He does not *live according to the truth,* which means that his attitudes, acts, and words are not under the control of his faith in God.

The gnostic approach was based on two fallacies which are always fatal for ethics. First, it isolated God from the arena of the human struggle. Second, it taught that salvation was the result of knowledge rather than of commitment to God.

The same errors are extremely prevalent in so-called orthodox Christian circles today. Many people connect God primarily with a building. They go to the church building to meet God. They dress in nice clothes and talk with appropriate words. Very few people would have the temerity to curse or tell an earthy story in the church building. They think of it as God's house, the place where God is. Religion becomes something that you do in a certain place, on a certain day, at a certain hour. It does not permeate all of life.

The barber shop is different from the church building. There is no conviction that God is there. The committee room where business decisions are being made is also off limits to God. These are ways in which people effectively isolate God from daily human existence.

Another gnostic tendency is to identify Christians as persons who believe certain things about God. In our churches we commonly give people a simple theological test when they present themselves for church membership. "Do you believe that Jesus is your Saviour, that he died on the cross, that he rose from the dead, etc." When the person answers in the affirmative, we baptize him, and he becomes a member of the church. You would think from this that Jesus gave such theological tests to people who were prospective disciples. But the truth of the matter is that he didn't. He challenged people to follow him. They were asked to take a radically new direction in life which brought profound changes to all areas of their existence.

Another idea is piously proclaimed by persons who do not understand the ethical demand of the Christian faith. They call for people just to preach Jesus and not be concerned about politics, economics, social problems, and the like. If you only listened to people like that and never read the New Testament, you might believe that the Bible really has nothing to say about injustice, hunger, poverty, the compassionate use of wealth, and the like. By limiting the gospel to what people like to call the spiritual, the Christian faith is divorced from business, politics, social justice, and other areas of our lives in the world.

One of the reasons why so many young people are disenchanted with the moral codes of their elders is that the hypocrisy and inadequacy of such approaches are so obvious. There is too much contradiction between religion and life.

The pattern for the Christian life is set forth in the phrase *as he is in the light*. *He* refers to Jesus. The moral tension under which the believer is to live is the life of Jesus. He is the fullest expression in history of what it means to live a responsible moral life under God.

The Christian, therefore, is to *walk in the light*. It is of course clear that our author does not suppose that the Christian will rise to the quality of life manifested in Jesus.

In this case, what does it mean for the Christian to *walk in the light?* It seems to me that it implies that the believer will take morality seriously. However close or distant they may be from their ideal, the least common denominator of all Christians is that they want to be good.

The moral quest of the Christian is a positive one. He is not concerned with discovering what he can get by with. Rather, he is dedicated to discovering what it means to be a follower of Jesus in his particular set of circumstances. Some people spend a lot of time trying to catalogue attitudes and acts so that they can determine which are neither illegal nor sinful. They feel that anything not included in those categories is permissible. It goes without saying that the moral character of their lives will be inferior to that of the person who earnestly wants to be and do good in a positive sense.

In the second place, to walk in the light means that the Christian accepts the life of Jesus as the moral imperative under which he lives. The insight characteristic of the moral temper of our times saying that moral codes are inadequate as standards for life is a valid one. The clue to morality for the Christian is not a code but a person. Morality is always an intensely personal matter. No other person can anticipate or understand the complexity of my moral struggles. Consequently, no one else can draw up an exhaustive set of rules that will be satisfactory for my life. The experience and support of others are helpful and necessary. But I live before God as a person with the responsibility of trying to be exactly what I ought to be under God. Since I am different from any other person, the pattern of my life cannot conform to a stereotype. It is only when I am truest to myself in the highest sense that I am really responding to the challenge of Jesus.

In the third place, walking in the light means that the Christian is honest with God and himself. He is not trying to hide his problems and weaknesses. He does not pretend that he is something that he is not.

The text says that people who walk in the light have *fellowship with one another*. They share in a common life and a common commitment. But more than that, having faced up to God and to themselves and having found the courage to be honest about their weaknesses and sins, they can be honest with one another.

Fellowship is impossible as long as we pretend that we are something which we are not. People often cast us ministers in the wrong role. They think of us as "holy men." Now the fact of the matter is that I am not a holy man, so I am tempted to hide this fact by playing the role of the holy man. I can dress in certain kinds of clothes, hold my hands in certain pious ways, and say pious things in a holy tone. This becomes a wall behind which I hide my needs and sins.

People also are inclined to play the same kind of game with us. They feel that they must not allow the "holy man" to know how they really think and what they really do. There is no possibility of genuine fellowship so long as we indulge in this kind of "make believe." It is only when we take down these walls that we can help each other become better than we now are.

Believers who walk in the light have the assurance that the *blood of Jesus his Son cleanses us from all sin*. The background of this symbolism is the significance of the blood of sacrifices in purificatory religious rites. The truth of the matter, of course, is that very little blood was actually shed in crucifixion. Even if nailed instead of bound to the cross, only a small amount of blood flowed before coagulation took place. Death usually came through shock, suffocation, and exhaustion.

The phrase the *blood of Jesus* refers to the life that was given. The writer identifies the Jesus who died as the *Son* of

God, in contrast to the teachers who denied that God could have any relation to the human Jesus. Jesus' giving of his life is central to the Christian understanding that the unlimited grace of God is available to sinners.

The verb *cleanses* is present tense in Greek. The present tense denotes continuous action. A more appropriate translation is "keeps on cleansing." That is, God's grace in Jesus Christ is the continuing answer to the guilt of the believer. Fellowship and cleansing, therefore, are the blessings that belong to people who walk in the light.

The Problem of Guilt
1 John 1:8–10

What is the believer to do about sin? To begin with, he should not deny it. Repression is not the answer to the problem of guilt.

Evidently the gnostic teachers held that as spiritual men saved by their knowledge they were above sin and incapable of being touched by it. Anyone who declares that he lives above sin is in an illusory world of unreality. Furthermore, such an attitude shows that the *truth is not in us,* for the truth in us will help us to face up to the reality about us. This same theme is repeated in verse 10. There the denial of sin is equated with blasphemy, for it in effect makes a liar of God.

Instead of denying our sins, we should *confess* them. But what does it mean to confess our sins? We should understand at the outset that confession is not a pious work by which we merit forgiveness. The follower of Jesus must resist the pervasive, continuing tendency to turn religious acts into pious works by which personal goodness may be measured. In Jesus' day prayer, fasting, and charitable gifts were used in this way (Matt. 6:1 ff). Tithing and attending religious activities might have been substituted for this triad if Jesus were speaking to our churches today.

Certain groups have made a practice of conducting regular services of public confession. In these services members are supposed to confess their sins to one another. Of course, the truth of the matter is that they never tell it all. No one in his right mind would dare make all his sins and weaknesses a matter of public record. In fact, it would be a very foolish act to do so. If in any congregation all the members publicly confessed all their sins, any number of homes would be destroyed, the church would be ruined, and the community would never recover from such an experience.

A further problem is that such practices may lead to a feeling of moral superiority. We may be tempted to feel that we are better than the other people who have not confessed. A seminary student who participated in the Mardi Gras festivities in New Orleans afterward felt a deep sense of guilt because of it. He felt constrained to confess to the church that he had sinned. Thereafter, he used this experience repeatedly as an illustration. He was extremely proud of his confession. Whenever a person does something that makes him feel morally superior to his fellows, to that extent he lessens his sense of need for God's grace. Salvation and forgiveness are from the first to last the work of God's grace. Nothing that we do cleanses or liberates us from guilt. Only God can do that.

Furthermore, programming confession robs it of the spontaneity and individuality which are characteristic of true confession. Confession must arise from within because of personal need and not be produced by pressure from without. The community should not program confession; it should seek to create the spirit of acceptance and love that makes confession possible.

Basically, it seems to me that confession involves two factors. First, it requires us to be honest in facing up to ourselves. So much so-called confession is superficial at best and unmitigated hypocrisy at worst, because people are not willing to see their real needs. The deeply prejudiced person who confesses his failure to perform certain prescribed religious duties is a case in point. So also is the example of the individual who prays weekly in a bland, general way, "Forgive us all our many sins," but who is unwilling to see that his greatest sin is his worship of things and unfeeling attitude for people who do not have the necessities of life. In the second place, confession involves a recognition that we cannot bear the burden of our guilt alone. It is a poison that destroys our peace and saps us of our creative energy. Someone else must be called in to help us with this burden.

There are times when we need to confess our sins to the group. Especially is this true if our actions have injured the fellowship of the community. Also, we need to confess our sins to persons whom we injure. It is not enough to tell God that we have wronged someone; we must tell the person who has been hurt also.

There are times, too, when we have a deep need to tell another person about our sins and problems. The brother who hears our confession enters into our guilt with us and helps us to bear the load of it. When someone else knows us as we are and, nonetheless, is able to accept us and forgive us—this becomes a concrete expression of the possibility of forgiveness. In this way a forgiving individual or a forgiving community can become the mediator of God's forgiveness.

But our sins constitute a rupture of our relationship with

God, the very source of our being. Alienation from God is the basis of our inner hostility and divisions and of our disturbed relationships with our brother. The incredible fact of the gospel is the declaration that God invites us to turn the burden of our guilt over to him. So confession in the final analysis means that we turn our sins over to God. I cannot atone for my sins, I cannot liberate myself from them, I cannot bear the guilt of them. So I turn them over to God.

In order to have a complete experience of forgiveness, however, the penitent must have the courage to believe that God genuinely forgives sins and loves sinners.

In every Christian community there are persons who still carry the guilt of past sins. Perhaps it is a foolish teen-age love affair concealed from husband or wife that constantly haunts the individual. It has long been recognized that the cause of a large amount of the emotional illness so common in our society is this problem of unresolved guilt.

Some emotionally ill people, burdened with the guilt of some act or thought, have confessed and confessed and confessed. But they have not found a solution for the deep anxiety that troubles them. Instead, they are still haunted by the wrong that they have done. What is the problem? They have not dared to believe that God can and does forgive people who are as unclean and evil as they feel themselves to be. They have the idea that God is against sinners. They are unable to believe in grace; they cannot accept the incredible fact that God is *not* against them!

Sometimes we Christians are to blame for this. We know so little of grace, love, and acceptance. We are often so unforgiving. We tend to shut people out who do not measure up to certain standards. The church frequently stands as a psychological barrier between a person and God, shutting him off from the forgiveness that he so desperately needs. Sometimes this starts in the earliest years in Sunday School when the thoughtless Sunday School teacher or parent tells the child: "God doesn't love you when you are bad." If this is true, there is of course no hope for any of us.

The text affirms that God is *faithful* and *just* with the result that he forgives our sins and cleanses us from all unrighteousness. We are not forgiven because we confess, because we deserve to be forgiven, nor because of who we are. We are forgiven because of who God is. He is a loving and forgiving God. If he failed to forgive us, he would be acting contrary to his nature, i.e., would be unjust and unfaithful. The TEV (Good News Version) gives an excellent translation of verse 9: "We can trust him, for he does what is right."

Often our hostility toward others expresses our conviction that God does not really love "bad" people. When we are harsh in our judgments, criticism, and condemnation of other people, we are simply saying that we do not understand what love and grace are. The truth of the matter is that I can never really believe that God loves me until I also believe that he loves you. I cannot believe that God is willing to forgive me unless I also believe that he is willing to forgive you.

An experience in depth of God's forgiveness brings about a breathtaking spiritual liberation with implications for all of life. I do not have to be against you, and I do not have to be against myself, since God is for all of us. God's grace frees us, therefore, from the shackles of prejudice, hatred, and contempt. If we ever really accept it, our energies and capacities are released, enabling us to live a creative, reconciling life in the midst of the tensions, hatreds, and divisions of our world.

Demand and Grace
1 John 2:1-2

The writer has already made it abundantly clear that the believer is a sinner, needing daily the cleansing, renewing grace of God. One way that we can deal with guilt is to lower the standards, thereby lessening the tension between what we are and what we think we ought to be.

But there is no tendency at all in 1 John to lessen the demand of the gospel. We are kept constantly under the absolute moral tension of the character of God as expressed in the life of Jesus. There is no condoning of laxity, no resorting to the kinds of excuses so commonly heard, such as: "After all, it is only human to do wrong." First John is written not to open the door to excuses for wrongdoing, but to point Christians toward the ultimate goal of their pilgrimage. In the phrase *that you may not sin,* the aorist tense of the Greek verb makes the point emphatic. It means "that you may not sin even once."

But the gospel is always demand and grace. Without demand, grace would be cheap sentimentality. Without grace, the demand would be an intolerable burden that would drive us to despair. When we are confronted with the demand of the gospel, we are made aware of our failures. We desperately need the word of grace at the moment that we honestly face up to our failures. So he has to add: *But if anyone does sin.* Again the tense is the aorist and the meaning is: "If anyone does commit a sin," that is, "sins at any point."

Note that the writer now changes the person of the verb

abruptly. When he talks about what Christ has done for sinners, he unconsciously includes himself. It is an artless indication that he is aware that he needs grace as much as the people to whom he writes. He is not arrogantly talking down to sinners. Instead he invites them to share God's grace with him.

The important point for the sinner to remember is that he is not abandoned in his sin. God loves us when we are not good. The sinner is not cut off from God by his sin, for he has an *advocate*.

Advocate is the translation of *parakletos* (paraclete). Literally it means "one who has been called alongside." It was used to designate a person who was summoned in to give help, particularly a representative for the accused in court. The word is used with different shades of meanings in the Johannine literature. In John 14:16 the Holy Spirit is called the *paraclete* (Counselor in RSV). There the meaning seems to be helper. In this passage, however, the meaning is related to that of the person who pleads the case of the accused in court.

The metaphor should not be pushed so far, however, as to give a distorted picture of God. The role of Jesus is not that of placating an angry God who is in a corner pouting at sinners. This kind of theology does an injustice to the teaching of the New Testament. We cannot allow a biblical metaphor to become hardened into the dogma of a God divided against himself. Any point of view that destroys the unity of Father and Son must be rejected. "God was in Christ reconciling the world to himself" (2 Cor. 5:19). What Christ did, God did.

In this case, what does the figure of our text mean? It means that God himself identifies with the sinner. It means that we are not left isolated and helpless when we sin. God in love for us even when we are sinners provides the answer to our guilt.

Jesus is also the *expiation* for our sins. This word is translated "propitiation" in the KJV. This reflects the fact that the underlying Greek word is capable of two divergent meanings. It means propitiation if it is used to describe what man does to placate the anger of a hostile god. It is often used in this sense in pagan religions. *Expiation* is the meaning when what is described is what God does to deal with the problem of sin in people. It describes God's actions to erase or to cover sins. Clearly this is the meaning in the New Testament.

Since God sent Jesus, this obviously was not done to placate his own anger and hostility. He acted to overcome the hostility and resistance of man toward him. The barrier that needed to be broken down was in man, not in God. Man as a sinner had a problem that needed to be solved. Because God is gracious, the solution is forgiveness and reconciliation.

In Jesus God has taken the ultimate step to deal with man's sin. There is nothing beyond this. God does not offer varying solutions to the problems of different groups or ages. God is everywhere and always a gracious, forgiving God. Consequently, the expiation of Jesus is not limited geographically or temporally. It is for the sins of *the whole world*. World has various meanings in the New Testament. Here it has the significance of humanity in its rebellion against God, that is, all unredeemed people.

4

What It Means to Be a Christian

How may a person know that he is a Christian? This is an important question which 1 John attempts to answer at various places. Two problems had created the necessity for dealing with this issue. On the one hand, some people, too lightly and on the wrong basis, had claimed to know Christ. On the other hand, persons considered by the author to be genuinely Christian had been intimidated into doubting the reality of their religious experience.

There is a way to test our profession of faith, according to 1 John. How seriously do we take the teachings and the acts of Jesus as the moral imperative for our lives? The effect that his teachings have on us is an indication of our commitment to him.

One of the pervasive tendencies of our churches is to substitute an arid intellectual orthodoxy for the kind of commitment that the Christian gospel demands. The affirmation of certain theological propositions is considered satisfactory proof in certain circles that one is a Christian. Nevertheless, this may be little more than a kind of twentieth century gnosticism that divorces faith from life.

Taking Jesus Seriously
1 John 2:3–6

In Matthew 25:31 Jesus declared that God divides men according to the way that they react to human need, i.e., prisoners, the hungry, the naked, the sick. We need to realize that belief about Jesus is not an acceptable substitute for responding appropriately to the personal demand set forth in these words of Jesus. When we make theological orthodoxy the sole test of religious faith, we are left with a very comfortable gospel.

A person can keep building his personal estate, live his cozy life behind walls that insulate him from man's despair and need, and enjoy the products of his affluence. Just so long as he believes in Jesus, he is in good shape religiously. He can leave his air-conditioned home, drive his air-conditioned car to an air-conditioned church and worship a Christ insulated from the evil, disease, and dirt of the blighted areas through which he has driven. This is the kind of fallacy that our writer decries.

Of course, what one believes about Jesus is important. The gnostic teachers were wrong theologically in that they had driven a breach between the human Jesus and the divine Christ. For this reason, the words and actions of Jesus had no religious significance for them. A "plan of salvation" can also do the same thing by reducing Christianity to propositions about Jesus. The gospel is not whole unless it confronts prospective disciples with the demands Jesus makes of his followers.

First John calls the person a *liar* who says that he knows Jesus but has contempt for or neglects what he says. We remember that this word does not necessarily mean deliberate prevarication. Rather, it describes the person whose statements do not accord with reality. He is a deluded, mistaken person who lives in an illusory, dream-world. *The truth is not in him* is simply another way of saying the same thing. Truth is the equivalent of that which is real or genuine as opposed to the false and illusory.

The phrase underlying the RSV translation *love for God* in verse 5 is ambiguous. It can either be translated "love of God" or "love for God." In the former the meaning would be the love that God has for the person. God's purpose in forgiving and claiming sinners is the complete transformation of their character and the elimination of all rebellion and disobedience. In the words of 1 John God wills to shape the believer's life by the teachings of Jesus. The more our lives are so shaped, the closer does the love of God come to reaching its goal in our lives. To say that the love of God is perfected is to say that it has achieved its desired purpose in a person's life.

But *love for God* may be the correct interpretation. In this case, it is the believer's love for God that constrains him to take the teachings of Jesus seriously. The closer he comes to the goal of living according to those teachings, the more he gives evidence of the completeness or perfection of his love for God.

It is the total life of Jesus that provides the standard for the Christian's life. Not only what he said, but what he did is important. Therefore, the writer affirms that the believer should *walk in the same way in which he walked*. The teachings of Jesus cannot be divorced from his life. Jesus taught that his followers should live in total dependence upon God and completely under his rule. By his actions he showed concretely what this meant. Without the illustration of the life, the teachings would not have the force that they have. Nor would they be complete.

What this means is that the Gospels are the center of the New Testament. They are the witness that we have to the kinds of things Jesus said and the kinds of things he did. If we want to know what it means to be Christian, we have to live with the Gospels. But we also must remember that the demand of the gospel is for us to live as Christians in the twentieth century. A valid Christian belief takes both the New Testament and the modern world seriously.

Loving, Not Hating
1 John 2:7–11

To this point the writer has been talking in rather general terms. Now he becomes much more specific, as he tells us what it means to live by the commandments of Jesus.

Perhaps we have been prepared for him to give us a list of things that Christians are not supposed to do—a moral code which contains all the "thou shalt nots" of the Christian life. Our tendency is to define goodness in negative terms. To be good is not to be bad; to be moral is not to be immoral. Many times mothers will say: "My son is a good boy. He neither drinks nor smokes." I always have the temptation to ask what he does, because the positive aspect of morality is much more important than the negative.

There have even been some religious sects that have taught that 1 John requires the Christian to live above sin. Then they define this in something like the following ways: the Christian is not supposed to drink, dance, attend movies, curse, or smoke. A woman is not supposed to wear lipstick or cut her hair. Of course the only way that you can hold to a doctrine of sinless perfection is to define morality largely in negative terms. This makes holiness and goodness attainable.

People who have leadership roles in churches tend to define morality with reference to practices which affect the institution. I frequently hear theological students single out certain members of their churches for praise. Almost with-

out fail I can predict how they are going to describe these
members. More often than not they say: "He comes to
church and he tithes." Search the pages of the New Testament as we may, we shall not find there this definition of
what it means to be a good Christian.

One of the strange contradictions of Christian history is
the way Christian groups have used the gospel to establish
another brand of pharisaism. That is, they advocate exactly
that approach to morality and goodness which Jesus opposed. Jesus incurred a great deal of wrath because he
challenged institutional morality and negative moral codes.

The problem with negative moral codes is that they only
make morality too easy. People who live according to such
codes are apt to have a sense of moral pride and to look
with contempt on people who do not live up to their standards. An oversimplified division exists between "good" and
"bad" people.

The good people are the ones who do not drink, dance,
smoke, or whatever the prohibited actions may be.

The bad ones are those who do.

By way of contrast the positive ethic of 1 John is based
on love. This is because being a Christian is conceived of
basically in terms of relationships—our relationship to God
and to one another. The central desire of Jesus for his
followers is expressed in the command for them to love one
another. This is where being good begins. Any concept of
morality or ethics that has another point of departure is
unworthy of the life and teachings of Jesus.

This is not a *new commandment*. The writer stresses the
fact that he is not introducing something novel into the
Christian gospel. He is simply calling their attention to a
commandment that Christians had received from their

Lord. They had it all along, from the very beginning of the Christian gospel.

But this old commandment is also *new*. It is ever contemporary, representing the will of the church's Lord for every new disciple. It is never outmoded. No new teaching can substitute for it. In the sense, also, that it is the basis of life for the Christian community in the new age inaugurated by Jesus Christ, it is new. The old age is characterized by prejudice, hostility, and greed. For people to really love one another in a sacrificial and self-giving way is a testimony that something new is occurring in the old order of things.

The commandment is *true in him*. It is in Jesus first of all that Christians have come into contact with true or genuine love. In Jesus God's love for man has come to its fullest and highest expression. Furthermore, it is true *in you*, i.e., in the Christian communities. In their love for one another which is in fact an expression that God's love is in them, Christians also show this genuine concern.

Because the darkness is passing away expresses the confidence of the writer in the future. Darkness describes the forces hostile to God. It is characterized by hatred, dissensions, divisions, prejudice, and all the emotions and forces that set man against man. But the future does not belong to the powers of hate and selfishness. The genuine light shining in the midst of the world because of God's love seen in the brotherly love of the Christian communities is a prophecy of the shape of the future. Light will gain the victory over darkness. This is simply another way of saying that love is stronger than hate, that forgiveness is more powerful than vindictiveness.

A very serious question pushes forward at this point. What if the group that calls itself the church is not characterized by a fellowship of love? What if it is divided by the same prejudices and hostilities that divide the world? What does such a church say to the world? Is it not a convincing witness that the gospel we preach is empty, that God's grace does not really change people and make them open, accepting, and loving?

It would seem so, would it not?

Again the point is made that there must be coherence between our profession and our practice. When we are *in the light,* we love our brothers, for this is what being in the light means. The false teachers in Asia Minor claimed to be in the light in the sense that they had received divine illumination. But they did not understand the ethical connotations of a genuinely illuminated life. Instead of loving people, they treated them with contempt.

The person who loves his brother is no *cause for stumbling.* Love makes people sensitive to the well-being and needs of others. When we love someone, we cannot act or speak selfishly without reference to his welfare. Therefore, what we do will not result in harm for him.

Love for the brothers, therefore, is genuine evidence that a person is actually in the light. Conversely, hatred for the brother is incontrovertible proof that a person is still *in the darkness.* This is true no matter how religious his language or how orthodox his theology. In the first instance, life is lived in confidence and security. It has a sure and certain goal, for love always gives direction and purpose for living. In the latter case, the person blinded by his hatred has no real sense of direction. Having shut his brother out of his life, he has also shut God out. Therefore, he has no real future. Hatred, prejudice, and lovelessness are always disastrous. They are harmful to the person toward which they are expressed. They are even more harmful, however, to the person who harbors them.

Now we can understand how demanding the Christian ethic really is. It is much easier to go to church services than to love the people who are there with us. It is easier to tithe (especially if we can get along well on 90 percent of our income) than it is to accept our brothers of another race or social class in our fellowship. But it is exactly this kind of love and acceptance which flows from a genuine relationship with God in Christ.

Responding to the Truth
1 John 2:12–14

Is it not rather foolish to expect people to love one another? We find so many people difficult to love because their ideas conflict with ours, or they have habits, characteristics, and attitudes that make it difficult for us even to like them. There is so much hostility and anger even among people who belong to the same family, club, or church. The problem is even more acute when factors like race and class are involved.

History teaches us that people of different races, countries, and social and economic classes often have difficulty even tolerating one another. It is rather too much to expect that people will be able to unload their baggage of suspicion, selfishness, and prejudice that determine to such a great extent their social relationships, isn't it? Is it not somewhat impudent for anybody to write to a group of people to tell them how they ought to think and act? Or, to preach to a congregation, for that matter, to tell them that they ought to open their lives and their circle of fellowship to include people that their social and racial circles reject?

After all, it is my business who I invite to my home, who I spend my time with, who I want my children to go to school with, isn't it?

The writer of 1 John does not base his appeal on his own ecclesiastical authority. He evidently was a respected Christian leader, but he does not call for his readers to heed his word because of who he is. Rather, he makes his appeal to them on the basis of their own religious experience. The only reason that he has the courage to expect of them what would not be expected normally of any group of people is his conviction that they have a relationship with God that has changed their lives. *"I am writing to you, little children, because your sins are forgiven."*

Little children know God in the forgiveness of their sins. It is not clear whether *little children* designates members of the community of a certain age group or simply refers to those who are beginners in their religious experience. Children in the faith may not have a profound grasp of theology. Their faith may be simple and naïve. But they have confidence that there is no barrier between them and God. They believe that God loves them, and they love him in return. Because of their own experience, they know what it is to be loved and accepted. Therefore, they are equipped to be loving and accepting.

These spiritual children also *"know the Father"* (v. 13). This means that they recognize that God is their father. They accept their status as children, which involves their willingness to depend on God. This dependence is based on the assurance that he will provide for their needs as a loving Father. Because they know God as Father, they also are aware that they are members of a family composed of God's other children, all of whom are their brothers and sisters.

Fathers know him who is from the beginning. Perhaps the implication is that age and experience in the Christian faith give one a basis for the more profound understanding and assurance that the years can bring. When a person trusts God through the years and finds his faith adequate for the trials, sorrows, and difficulties of life, he becomes more and more convinced that he is secure in the hands of the Eternal. The confidence expressed in Psalm 23 is the product of years of meaningful, reassuring experiences with God: "The Lord is my Shepherd, I shall not want."

Young men have overcome the evil one. An outstanding characteristic of the faith of young people is its victorious quality. Much is said in derogatory fashion about the young —their lack of moral direction, their rebellion, and the like. Older generations have been saying these kinds of things about young people through the centuries.

They say them today.

But, if you want to find a follower of Jesus who is willing to go anywhere, do anything, suffer any privation, and completely give himself in service for humanity, you are more likely to find him among the young. It is no accident that most mission and Peace Corps volunteers are from the young. This selfless commitment of young people has been characteristic of the Christian movement from the beginning. Contrary to the false image that we have of the first disciples, they were all evidently young men when they began following Jesus—some of them very young.

Overcoming the evil one is tantamount to overcoming hate and hostility. According to 1 John, these wrong attitudes toward others are the result of the domination of evil in the life. When a person overcomes the evil one, he is free to love. Once again we can note that young people are remarkably freer of prejudice and dislike than are their elders.

The principle message of the paragraph is clear. The writer is addressing his readers because they are Christian. Since they are Christian, he is confident that they will respond to the truth of the gospel. This quality of responsiveness to the real meaning of the gospel is one of the paramount qualities of genuine Christians.

Why can we be expected to love the unlovable or accept the unaccepted? There is only one answer. Because in personal experience we know a God who loves us, although we do not deserve his love. Therefore, we may dare to believe that true followers of Jesus will swim upstream against the currents of prejudice and selfishness that characterize society in general.

5

This World and the World to Come

There are people who think that anything which brings pleasure or enjoyment has to be sinful. This results from a misunderstanding of and a twisted attitude about life in the *world*. To begin with, we need to understand that the Bible speaks about the world in a number of ways.

The world may refer to this physical planet or to the universe with its myriads of planets and stars. The Christian view of the world in this sense begins with the conviction that God created it. The Genesis account affirms the essential goodness of all that God created. It also affirms that what God created was designed for man's responsible use and enjoyment.

The Christian and the World
1 John 2:15–17

There is absolutely nothing wrong, therefore, with having the things of the world which are essential for life. There is no sin involved in providing food, clothing, housing, and education for our children. There is something immoral, of course, when people are starving while we are overeating. We are told that the contents of the average American's

garbage can could feed a family of six in India. That kind
of inequity is terribly wrong.

Furthermore, it is not wrong to enjoy what God has
given us. Jesus himself apparently attended parties quite
often. He thought that a big party was an appropriate
response to the homecoming of the prodigal son. Too often
in the past the church has viewed gaiety, laughter, dancing,
etc. with great suspicion. In so doing, it has shut itself off
from those people who knew that this approach to life was
perverted.

In 1 John, however, *world* is used in a different sense. It
does not refer to God's created world but rather is a desig-
nation of the forces hostile to God. In this usage it is the
equivalent of this present evil age that is to be superseded
by the age to come. We are not to understand world as used
in 1 John in a geographical but a spiritual sense. This
meaning is made explicit in the (New English Bible)
translation of verse 15: "Do not set your hearts on the
godless world or anything in it."

Love for the world is the equivalent of being in rebellion
against God, of being allied with those forces that oppose
God. Our writer understands that people are confronted
with but two possibilities: either they are in fellowship with
God or they are hostile to him. In the terminology of 1
John they either love God or they love the world. There is
no neutral ground on which a person can stand.

"Things in the world" does not refer to the things that
God made. The phrase may better be understood as "that
which is included in the sphere of forces hostile to God."

"Lust of the flesh" is identified as one of the things
belonging to the godless world or sphere. *Flesh* is another
of those words used in different ways in the New Testament.

In the affirmation, "the Word became flesh," the writer means that Jesus was a real human being of flesh. Although the body may be used in the service of evil, it is not itself evil. Neither are the natural desires of the body for food, drink, sex, etc. evil. Because this has not been seen clearly, the pernicious idea that desires of the human body are evil persists. This has led to a denial of the natural functions of the human body such as sex. If the desires of the human body are indeed evil, then God has played a terrible trick on us by making us as we are. But *flesh* is used here and in other places in the New Testament to describe man in his alienation from God. The desires that belong to the world, therefore, are those that arise from a source that is opposed to God. These are *lusts of the flesh.*

Our writer also speaks of the *lust of the eyes* and the *pride of life* as belonging to the world of rebellion against God. The inordinate, irresponsible desire for things is not inspired by God. The spirit of evil and disobedience to God is its source. This spirit produces a wrong sense of values and an uncontrolled passion to satisfy it.

It is not the use of things but their misuse that is evil. It is not things but rather the worship of things as the supreme good or ultimate goal of our lives that the Christian faith condemns. This is the kind of idolatry which is so pervasive in western secular culture.

In the biblical order of priorities we are to love God, love people, and use the world responsibly. The problem is that we turn the order around. We love things and exploit God and people. This is a sin from which religious people are not exempt. I visited on one occasion in the home of the president of a missionary society. It was very noticeable that the stables for her horses were superior to the houses for the people who tilled her land. Far too many women spend their money on mink coats rather than to feed starving children. Too many of us prefer to have the newest, fastest, most powerful automobile to using our money in ways that Christian compassion dictates. These are expressions of *lust of the eyes* and the *pride of life*.

The foolishness of such lust and pride arises from their limited and passing existence as well as from the superficial and temporary character of their satisfactions. The world, that is, this present age of evil, is *passing away*. It is on its way out, along with the desires that it inspires.

Man is more than a stomach to be filled and a body to be clothed. Automobiles, fur coats, swimming pools, and automatic gadgets are very poor gods. They do not satisfy the deep needs and longings of the human heart. Man is more than a sexual mammal. The temporary satisfaction of the sexual drive that fails to take into account the sacredness of human personality, both one's own and that of a person of the opposite sex, does not bring real fulfilment. Instead, it produces frustration, emptiness, and loneliness. The wrong use of things and the false fulfilment of desires cuts a person off from the possibility of meaningful deep relationships which are the very essence of what being human means. It is the failure to recognize this and to shape one's life accordingly that is called love for the world.

The man who loves things is filled with terror by the threats of the future. He knows that the day will come when his gods no longer will suffice. The anxious person is he whose gods, locked in a safety deposit box, fluctuate in value with the daily vagaries of the stock market.

The person who loves God and people, however, faces the future with bright hope and great expectancy. Christian hope is based on the confidence that relationships transcend the narrow limits of time and space, of birth and death. Whatever may be the shape of the future, there will always be God and people in it—and so there will always be love.

The Christian and the End of the World
1 John 2:18–19; 22–25

Early Christians lived in a highly charged air of expectancy brought about by the conviction that the end of the world would occur any moment. They believed that the period of time between the resurrection of Jesus and his coming in power would be brief. Recent developments in the churches had heightened this sense of expectancy for the author of 1 John. *"It is the last hour,"* he solemnly affirms.

Some nineteen hundred years have passed and history still continues. Consequently, we may conclude that those early believers were mistaken about the time of the end. But this could cause us to miss a most important point. The perspective from which they viewed time, history, and the future is the only one that is appropriate for Christians in any age.

The Christian view of history is based on the belief that God controls it. Time does not move in endless, repetitious cycles as the Greeks and others in the ancient world thought. It is moving toward a point fixed according to the purposes of God.

The purpose of God in history is the ultimate triumph of good over evil. The biblical confidence and hope is that the day will come when all rebellion and recalcitrance in the universe will be overcome. Then all things will be brought together in a harmonious whole in Jesus Christ under the sovereignty of God (cf. 1 Cor. 15:27–28).

What should be the Christian's attitude toward the present and future? Because we are human, we can never be sure that we shall have another moment of time. We all expect to die someday. That day may be ten or twenty years from now. But there is always the possibility that this is the last second of our lives. All that I know is that my heart just beat another stroke. I cannot be sure that it will ever beat again. The point is that mortal men can only be sure of the present moment. It is all of time that they really possess.

Furthermore, anything that can happen at any moment can happen in this moment of history. This present moment contains the possibility of being that moment when history is brought to a climax. Anything that God can accomplish in the future, he can accomplish right now. Therefore, each moment is, as it were, the last moment, when viewed from our contingent and limited vantage point. God alone is in charge of the future. Belief in God involves, therefore, our surrender of the future to him who alone can determine it.

We see by this that the Christian view of the future should call us from undue preoccupation with that which is under God's control to responsible living in the present. Each day that we have is a day that God has given us. Because it is God's gift to us, we should accept it gratefully and live it as responsible human beings.

Every day of our lives should be lived as though it were the last day; for insofar as we can determine, it is the last day. The Christian should always sense that the Lord is standing at the door and that it may open at any time to admit him who brings history to its fulfilment. Of course, the Christian should not live in cringing fear of the future. Rather, he should live each day joyously and victoriously. His confidence that God controls the future liberates him to live in the present in the security that belongs to him as a child of God.

For our writer the signal of the seriousness of the times was the presence of *many antichrists*. The *antichrist* is a common motif in apocalyptic literature. He is the personification of those forces that oppose Christ, often pictured as the leader in the final persecution of the church and the last desperate resistance against the rule of God at the end of history.

In 1 John the antichrist is identified in terms of the concrete situation confronting the churches. Instead of one, there are many antichrists. They are the false teachers who have denied the reality of the incarnation. For the first time the writer deals specifically with the group that has created such serious problems in the churches. They themselves were a part of the Christian community. However, they have now separated themselves from those who believed that Jesus is the Christ. We do not know if this is a formal separation or not. It may be that the writer considers the erroneous beliefs of the heretics to be a wall that divides them from genuine believers.

An endless procession of people through the last centuries have confidently asserted that they know who the antichrist is. He has been identified as political leaders, tyrants, and prominent religious figures of all kinds. The identification of the antichrist is usually accompanied by the claim that the end of the world is at hand. We should have discovered after so many centuries and so many predictions that no one is equipped to make them.

The truth of the matter is that there are always many antichrists. The antichrist is the spirit of perverse hostility to God that pervades every age. It expresses itself in many people and movements. Great German Christians came to believe that Nazism was an antichrist movement. There are movements of this kind in every society. Certainly ours is not free of such perverse opposition to God and his purposes. But there are no movements or developments in history that give anyone a basis for predicting God's free acts as the Sovereign Lord of history. The problem is that people are not content to trust God for the future. We want to know; we do not want to walk by faith. Because of this, any sensational, apocalyptic preacher can always find a hearing for his predictions and a following for his ideas. What we need to understand is that we cannot escape the contingencies and uncertainties of the human situation by any kind of clairvoyance. The best solution is calm confidence in God arising from the conviction that our future is in good hands. Our responsibility as human beings is limited to the present.

The person who denies that Jesus is the Christ is called *the liar* (v. 22). Such a denial is considered to be the basic lie. One can be mistaken or deceived about many ideas which are peripheral or unimportant. But the beginning of the knowledge of the truth is the recognition that Jesus is the key to truth. He is God's highest and clearest revelation to men. If we reject him, our whole perspective will be distorted and erroneous. Once we start at the wrong place, we can never be anything but wrong anywhere along the way.

But Jesus did not come to give us a store of facts about God. The purpose of his coming is to make a genuine relationship with God possible. He came that men might know God in direct and personal experience. God himself comes to man in Jesus. Therefore, a rejection of Jesus is tantamount to a rejection of God. That is why the author says: *"No one who denies* the Son has the Father" (v. 23).

Conversely, those who *confess the Son* possess the Father. Confession in this sense is the acknowledgment that Jesus is God's son. This is the message which the recipients of 1 John had *heard from the beginning* and to which they are called to be faithful. Their relationship with God in Jesus Christ is the ground of the *eternal life* which they possess.

As we have already seen, 1 John is a call to Christians to be faithful to their original experience and commitment. We must, however, make a distinction between the validity of the Christian experience and our understanding of it.

My initial experience as a Christian came very early in my life. It was the beginning of a relationship with God that has continued to be valid until this day. At the same time, I do not interpret that experience today in the same way that I did 25 years ago. I could hope that my understanding of it is much more mature today than it was 25 years ago. This does not mean that my initial experience was not genuine. But the truth is that a twelve-year-old boy can only make a decision on the basis of his understanding as a twelve-year-old.

Before they attend the seminary students are sometimes cautioned by well-meaning people: "Be careful not to let your studies change you." Tragically, there are people who go through a university or a theological seminary without being changed. But that should not be the case.

Because our understanding is limited, there is no point in our lives when we should cease to be open to new insights and corrections of our previous ideas. Our relationship to God should become ever more meaningful; our interpretation of it ever more mature. That which does not change in this relationship is God's presence and love, made possible in and through Jesus Christ.

The Christian's Teacher
1 John 2:20–21, 26–28

Scholars surmise that anointing was a part of the mystic rites of initiation practiced by the gnostic groups. According to their claims, the initiates received knowledge of God through this. Our writer counters the claims of the false teachers with the affirmation that believers have already been *anointed*. The KJV translates the phrase more literally: "Ye have an unction." Unction or chrism refers to the application of oil in connection with a religious rite.

Believers have been anointed by the *Holy One,* that is, by either God or Christ. Anointing clearly is a symbol of the spiritual experience that Christians had at the time of their decision to commit themselves to Jesus Christ, the Son of God.

Because of God's gift to them at their conversion they *all know.* The writer goes on to explain that they know the *truth.* The truth, of course, is the revelation of God in Jesus Christ and their new life of fellowship with him and with other believers.

The churches of Asia Minor had been disturbed and Christians had been made uneasy by the gnostic evangelists. These bearers of a new message had presented themselves to the churches with boasts of new insights and understandings of the truth, which challenged the very foundations of the gospel already received by the churches. They had evidently attempted to usurp the teaching functions in the Christian communities. Because they already had their teacher, the Spirit of God who dwelled in their lives through faith, the believers could dispense with the deceitful teachers. As it is phrased in verse 27, *"You have no need that any one should teach you."*

Passages like this have been misused to justify the kind of anti-intellectualism that still pervades some sectors of American religious life. It is important, therefore, to understand what the teachings in this section of 1 John mean for our lives today.

In the first place, an important insight is affirmed here. Knowledge of God is a gift from God. God is not an object to be apprehended through mental exercises. He is a person who makes himself known in revelation. The Christian faith is based on the conviction that God comes to man in Jesus Christ. Through Jesus Christ a relationship is established with God. In his personal experience with God, the individual receives the insights necessary for him to live a life that will be worthy of his new relationship.

Throughout the Bible we are taught that wisdom and understanding necessary for living according to God's purposes are gifts from him. As these terms are used in Scripture, they do not refer to the accumulation of factual knowledge. Wisdom is insight into the purposes of God. Understanding is the ability to react in the right way to particular circumstances and persons, that is, the capacity to interpret how one should act in the varying situations of life.

This kind of knowledge is very personal. It does not come to anyone secondhand. This does not mean that God does not speak to us through our brothers.

It does mean that the experiences of our brothers do not suffice for us. It is only in our own personal encounter with

God, however that may be mediated, that we can know him.

A second truth that 1 John emphasizes is that his knowledge or experience of God is available to every person. The gnostic systems divided men into varying categories, differentiating those who had superior spiritual capacity from those who had no spiritual perception at all. No doubt the gnostic teachers in the churches addressed in 1 John claimed that their knowledge of God was due to their own spiritual superiority.

But our writer affirms: *"You all know"* (v. 20). There are no gradations of Christians according to spiritual capacity. All Christians know God; and they know him in the same way, that is, through Jesus Christ. There is no spiritual elite in the Christian community, who qualify by their superior capacity to be God's favorites.

The Christian community must ever resist the temptation toward stratification. People who have superior educational and social advantages tend to look down on their fellow Christians. It is also common for a devastating kind of spiritual problem to develop among people who consider that they possess higher spiritual gifts or that they more nearly fulfil the requirements of their moral code. This kind of attitude makes Christian community impossible. Genuine Christian fellowship arises out of the awareness that God does not have any inferior children.

Some people, on the other hand, make the mistake of equating ignorance with spirituality. They have a deep suspicion of education, especially theological education. They believe that the spirit of God will teach a Christian all that he needs to know.

This point of view fails to do justice to the matter of the

individual's responsibility for all his faculties, including the mental and physical ones. Our minds are also a gift from God, and we do not honor God by failing to develop them as much as possible. Indeed, only Christians who develop their minds are equipped to perform certain specialized functions in the body of Christ.

Some of the greatest Christians that I have ever known had very little or no formal education. But they had deep insight into spiritual matters, an intuitive grasp of the meaning of the Christian life. I could hope someday to know God and understand his purposes as well as they do.

At the same time, these people would not be prepared to serve as pastors and teachers of the churches. In order to fill these roles, a Christian needs as much technical knowledge as he can acquire. Biblical languages, the geography of Palestine, the cultural and political situation in the first-century Greco-Roman world—these are important matters that one can only learn by the diligent exercise of his God-given mental faculties.

True enough, we can know all these things and still miss the more important knowledge, the kind that God alone can give us. But those who perceive most clearly the purposes of God also know that they can honor him best by the dedication of all their faculties to his service. They also love him with "all their minds."

The truth which believers have been taught is that fellowship with God is established by their relationship to his Son. It is interesting that the writer does not caution them to keep on believing something about Jesus but to keep on abiding in him (v. 28). The truth is, therefore, their experience at the present moment of an intimate relationship with Jesus Christ rather than facts about him.

The Christian life, however, consists of a number of paradoxes. One is the fact that the One whom believers know in a present experience is also the one whose coming they anticipate. Faithfulness to their relationship with him in the present is a guarantee that they will not shrink from him in shame at his appearing. At least one of the principal motivations for Christian faithfulness is the desire to please him who is our Lord. We do believe that the Christian life has both a present and a future. We should want to live for him in such a way now that there will never be any occasion for regrets in the future.

6

The Children of God

As we have already noted elsewhere, the moral imperative of the Christian gospel is founded on the conviction that God is righteous. First John teaches that a righteous God begets righteous children. For *born of him* it may be better to read "begotten of him." The word means either, but in English we speak of being born of the mother and begotten of the father. God, the Father, begets his children.

Free from the Power of Evil
1 John 2:29–3:10

The child of God *does right*. But does he always do right? Our author has already stated emphatically that a person who claims not to have sinned is a liar. Does he contradict himself in this passage? The problem is to some extent related to the meaning of Greek tenses, which is not so easily brought out in English translation.

In 1:8 we read: "If we say that we have [at this present moment] no sin," that is, not one sin, etc. In 1:10 the tense is perfect and the affirmation means: "If we say we have never sinned at any time." In the clause *"if anyone does sin"* of 2:1 the tense is aorist. The aorist tense in Greek basically denotes point action. The RSV translation brings out the meaning of the tense accurately. We may stress it a little more in this paraphrase: "If anyone does commit sin at any time."

All these affirm the fact that every individual has committed acts of sin in the past, at the present moment is in need of forgiveness for such acts, and in the future can be expected to commit further sins.

But the same author now at this point in the epistle states that the child of God *does right,* that *"no one who abides in him sins,"* that *"no one who sins has either seen him or known him,"* etc. In all these statements he uses the present tense. The present tense in Greek denotes continuous or habitual action. So the affirmations really mean "keeps on doing right, keeps on sinning," etc. In other words, the Christian may commit acts of sin, but he is not moving in the direction of evil. His commitment is to the good. Both the quality and the goal of his life are totally different from what they would be, were he not a Christian.

But let us never make the mistake of believing that God accepts us into his family because we are good. Quite the reverse is true. *"See what love the Father has given us!* The possibility of our being children of God is based completely on his unmerited, incredible love. This should be the antidote to any self-righteousness, feeling of superiority, or deprecation of others. If we are anything at all, it is because God loves us.

But the declaration that believers are now the children of God raises a perennial problem. Why do they suffer from misunderstanding, hatred, and abuse? The answer is found in the experience of Jesus. He was God's son but the world did not *know,* that is, did not recognize him. His sonship was veiled. People thought that they knew him. They identified him as the carpenter's son, a resident of Nazareth, member of a family known to all. But they were mistaken. Had they known who he really was, "they would not have crucified the Lord of glory" (1 Cor. 2:8).

Believers are also in the world incognito. *The world does not* recognize them either. If their enemies had known that they were really children of God, early Christians would not have been persecuted and killed. But because they live in a world that is blind to who Jesus really was, Christians should not be astonished when they experience the same fate. The problem is defined, therefore, as the blindness of a world that knows neither God nor his children. Many a person who has suffered for the cause of righteousness has found solace in the knowledge that he had this high privilege of sharing in the rejection and suffering of Christ.

Not only are we called the children of God. The name corresponds to the reality. *"We are God's children now,"* at this very moment, in these circumstances, and in spite of our humble, insecure situation in this world order. We are not given a vague, vacuuous hope for the future. The believer's confidence in the future arises out of the present reality of his experience. He knows God as a loving Father. He knows himself as God's child. He knows other Christians as his brothers and sisters. If such wonderful relationships and experiences are possible in the present, what glories does God's future hold for us? We cannot even begin to imagine, for *"it does not yet appear what we shall be."*

The Christian hope is that we shall see *him.* Does the writer have God or Christ in mind? Probably Christ, although it does not really matter, since the two are so closely identified. When we see him, *"we shall be like him."*

The tensions between what we are and what we ought to be will be resolved. The vision of Christ will be the climax of the believer's pilgrimage. To *"see him as he is"* will involve seeing exactly what it means to be the Son of God. In the light of this vision we shall experience the fulness of what it means for us to be the children of God. We have noted that the goal of the Christian life is to be like Jesus. But his followers always live with a sense of failure and incompleteness. Nevertheless, they have the confidence that they are on a pilgrimage whose goal is assured. One day they shall attain fulfilment when they shall become exactly what they ought to be as God's children.

We who know him now are urged on by the hope of seeing him fully. This is the dynamic for the Christian's moral life. Knowing that the culmination of our pilgrimage will be the vision of him who is righteous and pure causes us to strive to be like him now.

In other words, the Christian does not surrender to frustration and failure in the moral struggle. He does not say: "I simply cannot cope with the difficulties of living a Christian life. Therefore, I shall quit trying to do so." No, he continues to struggle upward under the imperative of the life of Jesus, desiring to be better each day than he was the day before. In the words of the writer, the Christian *purifies himself*.

Again the tense is present: he "keeps on purifying himself." The tense of the verb makes it clear that moral purity is not achieved in one ecstatic experience in this life. It is not accomplished by a single response to an altar call. The effort to realize fully the possibilities inherent in our relation to God as his children lasts throughout all the days of our lives.

Since sin is the contradiction both of the character and will of God as expressed in Christ, we cannot take it lightly.

Not only is God righteous; he also demands righteousness. The failure to be righteous, therefore, is *lawlessness*. It is a rebellious flaunting of the purpose of God for his creatures and of the divine order for the universe.

For the believer to live under the domination of evil is a contradiction. Jesus came to *take away sins*. The verb translated "to take away" means "to bear up." Here the idea is that Jesus came to bear up sins in the sense of lifting their power from man. He broke sin's dominion and made it possible for people to be liberated from its grasp.

Therefore, believers "do not continue to sin." This means that they are not enslaved by sin's power.

We have said that an understanding of the Greek tenses will help to resolve the apparent contradictions in the English text of 1 John. But in so doing, we may have left an erroneous impression. The truth of the matter is that none of us allows the gospel to manifest its total power in our lives. Consequently, there are always unredeemed areas in our attitudes and actions.

Let me make it clear where I think we can go wrong in our understanding of 1 John. Some people have taught and believed that an alcoholic, for example, could not be a Christian. They reason that the power of the gospel would liberate him from his slavery to drink. He could not be a Christian and "continue in habitual sin." We must concede, however, that the alcoholic is no more a contradiction to the gospel than most of the rest of us. The person who "continues to" gossip, to be prejudiced, or to be selfish with his money also "continues in habitual sin."

Only if we interpret morality as a circumscribed legalistic code, leaving out the kinds of sins that are exposed in 1 John, can we possibly claim moral perfection. It was on this basis alone that Paul could make the claim for pre-Christian Saul: "As to righteousness under the law blameless."

So there is never a time when we do not need grace, even after we have believed. But the thesis of 1 John is also true. The believer no longer lives under the power of evil but under the power of God. This means that there are new possibilities for dealing with the sins of our lives—possibilities, it is true, that most of us will admit have *not* become a full reality in our lives.

The key phrase in the whole passage is found in 3:8: *"For the devil has sinned from the beginning." Has sinned* is also a present tense in the Greek text, literally "keeps on sinning from the beginning." What it means is the following: From the beginning the devil's character is that of unrelieved perversity. There has never been anything but evil in his life. When evil rather than good is the dominant force in a person's life, he indicates thereby that he is a child of the devil.

Our author may think of that which he calls *God's nature* or, more literally, "God's seed" in us as that which lies outside the power of sin. If so, this idea is similar to that of the teachers whom he combats. But he also differs sharply from them. He holds that the children of God, those in whom God's nature dwells, will show their parentage by the quality of their lives in the world. Above all, they will be characterized by love for their brothers. In this last statement we see how our writer stands at opposite poles from preachers of a legalistic righteousness. He does not present a long list of "Thou shalt nots." His is a positive, dynamic righteousness, expressed first and foremost in the realm of human relations.

No man is righteous who does not have right relations

with his fellows. According to the Christian gospel, righteousness in human relations is not just seeing that everybody gets his due. It is a life of love that seeks to see that all men get more than their due, even as God has given us more than we deserve.

Free to Be a Brother
1 John 3:11–18

Brother—it's such a hard word to learn to say, more difficult still to live it. The gospel teaches me that I should substitute it for all those terms that I learned to call other people before I realized how much God loved them. All the names that express passion and prejudice, suspicion and selfishness, contempt and dislike must disappear from my vocabulary. They contradict the gospel and deny my relationship to God. My fellow believer, white or black, poor or rich, oriental, African, or South American, is my brother. The Christian community is a family whose existence and life are rooted in the will of the Father. From the very *beginning,* that is, consistently and always, his desire for his family has been expressed in the command: "Love one another."

The word brother evokes a variety of emotional responses. Warmth, tenderness, loyalty, constancy—these along with many other wonderful associations may be connected with it.

But there are also brothers who hate one another. Our closest relationships can be the source of our greatest joy or of our most tragic experiences. Brother can also mean evil passion, bitter jealousy, heartlessness, disloyalty. The primeval pattern of such sibling rivalry and hatred is the Cain-Abel relationship.

How does one explain this tragic story? Brothers they were—but not in the deepest sense. Cain *was of the evil one;* in the terminology of 1 John, his father was the devil (2:10). For our writer love and hate flow from two divergent sources. By his attitudes and relationships toward others, the individual reveals the source from which his own spirit is supplied. The proof of Cain's real parentage was unmistakable. He *murdered his brother.* The hostility of the evil man was aroused by Abel's goodness. There is a natural antipathy between evil and good. As a result, evil attempts to destroy goodness.

This is the tragic story of human history. The good man constitutes the conscience of evil society. Without his goodness, the evil of others goes unrecognized for what it is. But once evil comes into contact with goodness, it is shown to be evil.

Evil men can come to terms with a good man in various ways. There is always the possibility that a person will repent of his evil and turn to the good. But more often than not men who practice evil react to good men with murderous fury. The fate of prophets is tragically similar. On very few occasions has the response to them been repentance. Usually they have been destroyed.

Let us illustrate. In a society dominated by prejudice, the person who is accepting and loving to the outcasts generally is more hated than the outcasts themselves. Thus, in recent times, the white man who bore the label "nigger-lover" found himself in a more untenable position with the people of his own race than did the black man. Similarly, the black man committed to forgiveness and acceptance in his relationship with white people will find that he is an object of hatred and scorn in some segments of black society. This, of course, explains in large measure much of the hatred directed toward Jesus. When he went to eat with the despised Zacchaeus, "they all murmured" against him (Luke 19:7).

It seems to me that one of the vital measures of a church's validity is the way that it reacts to the prophets whom God sends to it. Far too many times have modern prophets suffered the fate of Amos in ancient Israel at the hands of religious institutions. An attitude of angry hostility toward the man whom God raises up to be our conscience puts us in the category of Cain. It throws the origins of the community's life in doubt, because Cain *was of the evil one*.

The Christian community is not to follow the example of Cain in their relation to their brothers. On the other hand, Christians are not to be surprised if the world hates them.

Insofar as it is a community of love, the church is the conscience of a divided, prejudiced, and oppressive society. The attitude of the world, i.e., man in his rebellion and antagonism toward God, is one of hatred toward the community that expresses the spirit of God. Of course, the church can come to terms with society by adopting society's structures, prejudices, and ideas. In such a case, the church no longer embodies the will of God for man but is an expression of forces opposed to his will. Society will feel comfortable with such a church; but God is not pleased with it.

How is one to be sure that he possesses the life that God gives (v. 14)? The answer is clear. Possession of life is expressed by love toward one's brother. At the opposite pole stands hatred which is murder. The spirit of murder is the absolute negation of the spirit that imparts life. We readily see that our writer is very close here to the teaching of Jesus in the Sermon on the Mount (Matt. 5:21–24).

In his day, as now, murder was understood as physical violence that resulted in the loss of life. But Jesus placed the person who felt murderous anger or contempt for another in the category of murderers. Five million Jews could never have been murdered by Nazis if the emotions of anger and contempt for them had not been cultivated first among German people. The Jews came to be regarded as less than human. When people are classified as animals, then the gas chamber becomes a logical solution to race problems.

By the same token slavery and post civil war suppression of minority groups in America would not have been possible in a truly Christian society. Because blacks were regarded with contempt, at best as useful tools, it was possible to exploit them.

The Christian is not supposed to hate. But neither is some kind of benign neutrality Christian. Many people feel that they are being Christian if they can say that they do not harbor ill-will toward anybody. The Christian, however, is to be for people. This is what it means to love our brother.

We are not allowed by the New Testament to interpret love as a kind of superficial sentimentality. The life of Jesus of Nazareth will not permit us to do that, for he gives to love its Christian meaning. *"He laid down his life for us."* That is what love means. It means that one is ready to make the ultimate sacrifice for the person who is loved. No man can do more for another than to lay down his life for him.

It is not at all clear what the theological significance of Jesus' death is. There are ransom theories, substitutionary theories, example theories of the crucifixion. No one has ever been able to give a complete and comprehensive statement about the meaning of Jesus' death that would interpret it satisfactorily. About the best that we can do is to use figures of speech. One mistake commonly made is to ascribe finality and infallibility to that which is always partial—that is, to our grasp of the reaches of God's grace. We see through a glass darkly. All our insights are partial, limited, contingent. We can only be thankful that we are saved by grace and not by our theology.

One affirmation is consistently made in the New Testament. Jesus died for us, whatever may be the limitations of the analogies used to explain this. First John spells out very clearly a Christian corollary to this belief. We ought to be willing to lay down our lives for our brothers on whose behalf Christ died.

How defective and sinful are our attitudes toward others! Church members still argue about whether they ought to accept God's children of a different race or class in their social circles. The truth is that if we were really Christian, we would not only be proud to sit with them, eat with them, work with them, play with them. We would also be willing to die for them.

There have been times and places when Christians did have to die for one another. More often this has not been necessary. How then is this love which is willing to offer up life itself to be expressed in everyday terms? The answer is simple: by performing those common sense, essential acts necessary to meet the needs of our brother. If he is hungry, he is to be fed. If he is without shelter, he is to be housed. If he is cold, he is to be clothed. If he is sick, he is to be treated. If he is ignorant, he is to be offered the possibility of education.

The person who *closes his heart* against his brother in need has failed the test that genuine faith in Jesus must pass. Some people will say: "I do not see any brothers in

need." No, and we can never see the need of others so long
as we drive from our air-conditioned homes in air-conditioned automobiles to worship in air-conditioned churches
and consider that our service to God.

They are with us—the hungry, the deprived, the disen-
franchised—in every city and region of this country and
across the world. There are enough of these brothers in need
to use all our superfluous good. We can find them if we only
tear down the walls that we erect to isolate ourselves from
the ugliness and destitution of our society.

It is easy to talk about love—or, for that matter, to write
about it. But it is awfully difficult to do love. It is in the
doing and not the talking that we show whether the richness
of God's love has banished the poverty of our own selfish
spirits.

Free from an Accusing Conscience
1 John 3:19–24

The Christian's assurance in his relationship to God is
subjected constantly to assaults from without and within.
Sometimes our accusers are other men. Because we do not
conform to their particular notion of what a Christian ought
to be, they question the authenticity of our faith. It is safe to
say that you are considered by some other religious group
or groups to be outside the circle of the redeemed, no
matter what the church or religious circle to which you
belong.

At other times our accusers are our own consciences. But
even this is not a private, independent source of judgment.
We need to understand that our own judgment of ourselves,
or in modern terminology, our self-image, may be determined to a great extent by the opinions held by other people

about us. Consequently, the voice of conscience may be only an echo of the prevailing ideas and value judgments of a particular social or religious group.

I have known any number of people who accepted the negative judgment of the religious community on them without question. They thought that the voice of the community was the voice of God. At other times, they accepted without question the voice of a preacher who had assumed the divine prerogative of judging and condemning as the voice of God. Their image of themselves conformed exactly to what the church members thought about them. They felt that they were worthless sinners, because this was the consensus of opinion held by the religious community. My own conclusion in many cases was that the rejected persons possessed more genuinely Christian qualities than did their self-righteous accusers.

The moral and religious values of the group are valid influences for shaping our conscience only insofar as they accord with the genuine message of the gospel. The truth is that every interpretation of the gospel must be kept under criticism because all our insights are partial and all our judgments are warped by sin. The more religious a group thinks itself to be, the more apt it is to be completely blind to the meaning to the gospel. And the more apt it is to contribute to the separation of man from God. This is the real lesson to be drawn from the sins of pharisaism.

When we have been reared in a negative, pharisaic moral environment, our consciences, shaped in that environment, may condemn us for the most trivial practices. For example, a lady reared in a perfectionist sect declared to me that she could not possibly become a Christian so long as she smoked and wore cosmetics. She had been taught to believe that such practices constituted an insurmountable obstacle to a relationship with God. Although she herself had broken away from her religious background in her own practices, her conscience continued to affirm the moral values of the religious community in which it had been shaped. The woman was convinced that God had the same attitude toward her that she had toward herself.

Science has proven that it is extremely foolish for people to smoke. By so doing, they will probably cut about eight years off their life span. Nevertheless, neither smoking nor the use of cosmetics says anything at all about a person's relationship to God, whatever effect they may have on his health. There are exceptionally good Christians who smoke, just as there are many wonderful, sensitive compassionate people who overeat and do many other things that are harmful to them personally. Also, there are cruel, perverse people who do the same things. But a person who has been taught to believe that practices of this kind are terrible sins may feel cut off from God if he engages in them. This is because the uninformed voice of a guilty conscience, which is really an echo of the judgment of a community, is misunderstood as the voice of God.

It is very common for adolescents reared in the church to have extremely difficult spiritual crises as the result of a guilty conscience. Often they become members of the church at a very early age. Then at puberty they begin to feel the powerful stirrings of hitherto unknown and strange forces. They feel differently about themselves and others. Too many times they have not had much help in understanding the complexities and potential of the human body. In fact, they may have been tragic victims of a warped moral code that considers sex to be dirty and sinful.

In such cases, they may be convinced that the strong, normal human urges that they experience are really evil. They may come to believe that a person who feels the way they do cannot possibly be a Christian. They are unaware that other normal adolescents have the same kinds of feelings and impulses.

This may explain why numbers of adolescents present themselves anew in our churches on profession of faith. It also probably explains why some of them will rededicate themselves to God repeatedly in services where they are called on to do so. These acts could represent their attempts to come to grips with the insecurity of a guilty conscience. Persons who work with young people need to be aware that the tensions of adolescence can produce religious insecurity and be prepared to help them to move toward assurance in their faith.

So many people have experienced terrible anguish caused by the sense of having been cut off from God by an impenetrable wall of guilt. But neither the judgment of our own conscience nor that of other men ultimately determines whether or not we are included in the family of God. This is done by God and God alone.

The real test of a believer's relationship to God is not the state of his conscience. In the preceding passage, the writer has affirmed that love flowing from God into the life of the believer manifests itself in concrete acts of love that meet the need of destitute, hungry, unfortunate brothers. This is the test that Christians need to be concerned about passing. It is not based on man's criteria; it is based on God's revelation of himself in Jesus of Nazareth. We must not substitute our criteria of a valid experience of God for that which he has given us.

Members of a community engaged in an active life of compassionate, self-sacrificing concern expressed in the name of Christ toward persons in need pass the test for genuine religion set forth in 1 John. They should not allow the insecurity of their consciences to undermine their assurance of a valid relation with God. *If their hearts do condemn them, they can reassure their hearts, for God is greater than their hearts.* In other words, God's acceptance of us is decisive for our acceptance of ourselves and not the opposite.

We have been discussing why the conscience cannot be trusted as an infallable guide in matters of our personal faith. We do recognize that there are times when the voice of conscience, especially if it has been liberated and informed by the power of the gospel, raises valid accusations against us. None of us would claim that his life and acts are always worthy of God's children.

A consciousness of unworthiness or failure produces a sense of guilt.

Although a guilty conscience may have nothing at all to do with the fact of our belonging to the family of God, it does disturb the quality of our relationship to our Father. Unquestionably, our sense of peace and joy in our Christian experience will be greater if we have a clear conscience, or, as our writer expresses it, *"If our hearts do not condemn us."*

The factor of guilt is disruptive in any of our relationships with the people who love us. The husband who has not betrayed the love and trust of his wife finds a greater happiness in his marriage than is possible otherwise. Most of us can remember when as children we were unfaithful to the trust of our parents. We also recall how such experiences disturbed and diminished the confidence and happiness of our lives in the home.

Others will join me in testifying that we have had similar experiences in our Christian lives. Some of our greatest periods of doubt and spiritual depression have coincided with those times when we have not been faithful to God. We tell ourselves that God loves us in spite of our betrayal of his love—which is true. But the fact remains that our faithlessness clouds our relationship to him. Conversely, our sense of his presence and our confidence in his love are strengthened when we are joyously committed to his purpose for our lives—*"If our hearts do not condemn us, we have confidence before God."*

Confidence before God is the basis of the Christian's security in this life. The gospel attempts to lead us to the assurance that we belong to a loving, capable Father who provides for our needs. The picture of the trusting believer is the little child who is secure in the knowledge that his daddy will care for him. He is not anxious about what he is going to eat or wear next month or next year. He knows that whenever a need arises he can go to his daddy who will provide for his welfare. Christians are supposed to find this kind of security in their confident, complete dependence on God.

Such confidence in God as Father prompted the affirmation: *"We receive from him whatever we ask."* This, of course, is not to be misunderstood. It is modified by a condition: *Because "we keep his commandments and do what pleases him."*

A statement like the one in our text does not mean that God is going to give us wealth, modern conveniences, success, or anything else of this nature just because we love and serve him. If Christian history teaches anything at all, it teaches that the very people who are most dedicated to doing the will of God are the ones who suffer most cruelly at the hands of the world. The appeals that are used to promote church financial campaigns are sometimes more pagan than Christian. Many people actually believe that God is going to make them more successful financially if they give to the church. The blessings of God cannot be construed in this sense from the point of view of the New Testament. We are called to a cross, not to financial success.

What this passage does mean is that God's faithful children will receive from him what they ask for as his children. What God's children want are opportunities to serve him, the insight essential if they are to do his will, the courage to acquit themselves nobly with credit to their Father in the difficult circumstances of life. When our requests to God arise out of selfish or evil motives, we are not praying to him in our character as his children obedient to his will.

For the writer of 1 John genuine Christian existence rests upon two bases: our acceptance of God who comes to us in Jesus Christ and our acceptance of our brother whom God has given us (v. 23).

As we have seen, the love that we have toward our brothers is expressed in practical, sensible, self-sacrificing acts that meet his need. Such an approach conforms to the example and teachings of Jesus. They are proofs that we "believe in the *name of his Son Jesus Christ*." They show that we are a part of the community of faith and love that God through Jesus brings into being. The love that believers have for one another in keeping with the commandment of their Lord arises from their union with God. It is an expression of the fact that they *abide in him,* that is, they draw their life from God, and that he abides in them, that is, God expresses his life of love through them.

Any judgment of the validity of our Christian experience that does not begin with the acceptance of our brother is to be rejected, according to 1 John. This is true whether it is the judgment of another person or of our own conscience. If we reject our brother, we have valid reasons for questioning the genuineness of our profession of faith. *"The Spirit which he has given us"* moves us toward love, forgiveness, reconciliation; not toward malice, prejudice, divisions.

7

The Test for Inspiration

Early Christians were not left with a memory only. The dynamic of their life is to be explained by their conviction that Jesus Christ who had walked among them in Palestine was still in their midst in his Spirit. God had not left them leaderless to face the new crises, problems, and questions that continued to arise. They had the revelation and inspiration of the Holy Spirit to enable them to find the right solutions and directions. This explains why the role of the prophet was so important in the churches of the New Testament. He was the person who had insight into the purposes of God and who proclaimed the messages inspired by the Spirit which gave direction to the church's life.

Let us look at inspiration.

Spiritual Inspiration
1 John 4:1–6

Church services apparently were very unstructured and dynamic. Any person who felt led by the Spirit could participate in the services by proclaiming a prophetic word. As Christianity expanded into the Gentile world the number of traveling missionaries and prophets increased. In any church service one or more of these visitors, some of them perhaps heretofore unknown to the congregation, might be present and were at liberty to present their own messages.

The claim was made by all these people that their words were inspired by the Spirit.

As can be seen clearly, this situation contained the possibilities of great confusion. An infinite number of widely divergent ideas could be proclaimed by persons who, sincere or otherwise, claimed to have received them by revelation from the Spirit.

Such was the case with the false teachers who denied the reality of the incarnation. They claimed the authority of the Spirit for their religious view. In fact, they must have taught that the fresh revelations they had received from God superseded the old, now outdated gospel originally received by the church members.

This situation has continued to persist through Christian history. Every generation has had its share of innovators who vow that they have received new revelations from God which correct or add to what God has previously revealed. On this basis, they proclaim theirs to be the complete and, therefore, authentic Christian faith. Very few members of our churches have missed out on the experience of having persons knock on their doors with the intention of helping them to know the "truth" which they are supposed to have missed.

Not only so, but preachers and teachers claim the inspiration of the Spirit for their messages. The average church member often finds himself perplexed because these messages are many times contradictory. One may believe, and rightly so, that God's Spirit does not inspire contradictions.

First John advises Christians to "put the spirits to the test." The verb *to test* referred to the process by which anything, such as a metal, or, in this case, an idea was examined to determine whether it was genuine or false. This process of testing was necessary because of the activity of deceivers or *false prophets*. We could add that the listener should be critical and discerning in any case, because even sincere people can be wrong in what they say.

We should quickly remark that a suspicious, paranoid attitude is certainly not Christian. Some people suspect every person that they meet to be a Communist or a heretic. The Christian is open, accepting, and trusting. At the same time, he is to exercise discernment as he listens to persons who claim to be bearers of God's word.

The truth of the matter is that no one of us who preaches the gospel is free from error. Consequently, no person should accept everything we say, no matter how much he trusts us and knows that we are trying to do and say the right thing.

People are also victimized at times by persons who use the Spirit as a club. If we want to put across a controversial program or idea, we can put those church members who oppose us at a terrible disadvantage by claiming that God is leading us in what we want to do.

The question arises: How are people to be put to the test when they declare that their ideas are inspired? The answer given in 1 John makes the incarnation the key. The Christian faith begins with the conviction that *"Jesus Christ has come in the flesh."* The Spirit of God does not lead, as the gnostic teachers claimed, to a denial of the significant role of Jesus in revelation. God's Spirit leads to the opposite conviction. The words and deeds of Jesus are pivotal for the Christian understanding of what God is doing in the world. This is based on the belief that what God does in any generation is consistent with what he did in Jesus.

This is a very important concept. Since Jesus is the Son

of God, he is the point of departure for our interpretation of God's acts in all of history. This was the principle used by early Christians in interpreting the Old Testament. For this reason they came out with an understanding of the Old Testament that differed widely from the doctors of the law, the acknowledged experts in Jewish writings and teachings.

The point is that early Christians did not find in the Old Testament a text and, then upon discovering that it had been fulfilled in Jesus, conclude that Jesus was the Christ, God's Son. In fact, their prior interpretation of Scripture was contradicted by what Jesus did—especially by the crucifixion. Rather did they proceed from the opposite point of view. They were convinced by the resurrection that Jesus was Christ and Lord (Acts 2:36). With this conviction they turned to the Jewish Scriptures to discover the coherence between what God had done in Jesus and what he had been doing in the history of Israel.

The same principle should also prevail as one tries to understand what happened after the incarnation. Jesus is the principle through which the New Testament must be understood. In a practical way this simply means that I cannot start with Daniel and Revelation in order to find the key for understanding Mark. This would be to start at the periphery rather than at the center. I must begin rather with the Gospel of Mark and move out from there. God's revelation in Jesus Christ is the clue to the interpretation of all Scripture. The Gospels are the witness to that revelation. This means that a historical, objective, serious study of the Gospels must be a primary concern of teachers and pastors who wish to help people to understand the meaning of the incarnation.

The same principle holds true with regard to other developments. There have been people who have declared on the basis of private revelations from God that the practice of polygamy had been sanctioned. I cannot accept this. I do not necessarily mean that I believe the person who makes such pronouncements to be insincere. He may sincerely believe that God has given him a divine revelation or vision. But because of what Jesus taught about marriage, I can never accept the principle of polygamy as the ideal for the Christian family.

Of course, the situation depicted in 1 John is an extremely serious illustration of the possibilities of this kind of error. On the basis of their revelations they had received through visions or otherwise, the heretical teachers were denying the very basis of the Christian faith by robbing it of its historical foundations in the life of Jesus. For this reason they are called false prophets and *antichrists*. By putting them to the test, Christians would find that they represented the spirit opposed to God which pervaded the rebellious world of hostility to God.

The success of the false teachers is easily explained. What they say is naturally attractive to the *world* because it proceeds from the same spirit that rules the rebellious world of enmity to God. The spirit that inspires their utterances is hostile to the Spirit that leads people to faith in Jesus Christ.

But the future of Christians is not determined by a majority vote. When shall we ever learn this? Having sold out to the pagan world and adopted its goals and standards of success, the institutional church finds itself defeated and frustrated by the computer. According to the latest polls, church attendance has fallen another percentage point in the past year. Now that ought to tell us something—about ourselves and our institutions. But it says nothing at all about God and the believer's future. The believer's future is guaranteed by the power and love of God who is the sovereign Lord of the future. Statistics have nothing to do with this.

"You are of God," says our writer, and *"have overcome them."* The truth was that the forces arrayed against the small, struggling Christian communities were immensely superior to them by any quantitative measure. But all reality is not immediately visible, nor can it be measured by our machines. Christians *have overcome* the forces hostile to them in spite of all appearances to the contrary. Their victory is first of all the victory of Jesus in his life, death, and resurrection. The power of God is there shown to be stronger than the forces that seek to frustrate his purposes.

Christians *have overcome* in their own experience. The world of hate, darkness, fear has no authority over them. They live in the light of God's love in a new fellowship of understanding and joy. On this basis they can look forward to the future with optimism. They know that light will conquer darkness. So our writer confidently asserts: *"He who is in you is greater than he who is in the world."* The mighty resources of God's power are available to the people who are following Jesus.

For the writer of 1 John the demarcation between *truth* and *error* was clear and unmistakable. The *spirit of truth* led one to commit himself to Jesus Christ as the crucial revelation of God's love and grace. The *spirit of error* inspired those who were hostile to Jesus.

8

Why Love Our Brother?

We read here again the argument that has now become familiar to us. God is the source of love. When we possess the life that flows from him, we express its essential character by our love for the children of God. The absence of love is an undeniable indication that there is no real connection between the individual and God, *because God is love.*

We cannot turn this affirmation around to say: "Love is God." The absence of the definite article before *love* and its presence before God in the Greek text prevents us from so understanding it. But even apart from the grammatical structure of the clause, we know that the author does not conceive of God as a virtue or a principle.

God Loves Us
1 John 4:7–18

Neither is the verse an attempt to define how God is actually constituted, which would be an exercise in futility. What God actually is lies far outside our ability to comprehend or define. But the affirmation *God is love* defines the way that God relates to people. The conviction that God is love arises out of one's own personal experience of being loved and accepted by God. Such a faith expresses the fact that God relates to us in an extremely personal way. It puts Christianity where it belongs—in the context of personal relationships. What it means to be a Christian is defined in terms of our relation to God and to others rather than in terms of the isolated negative kinds of virtues that we may possess.

Love, therefore, is the one absolutely indispensable ingredient in a Christian's life. We can be virtuous, religious, honest, faithful to the church, and possess any number of other excellent qualities. But if love is missing, we cannot be characterized as Christian (cf. 1 Cor. 13:1–3). The most religious, respectable, virtuous people of his day were exactly those indicted by Jesus as being furthest from the kingdom of God. The problem was that they were also self-righteous, harsh, judgmental, and lacking in compassion. Religion tends to make people like this—even the Christian religion, if the genuine spirit of love is not exalted to its central and controlling place.

But what do we mean by love? The word is used to refer to such a wide variety of emotions and attitudes. What people call love is often nothing more than cheap sentiment, the desire for self-gratification, unrealistic romanticism, or blatant sensuality. The word signifies whatever is understood by the person who uses it or hears it.

Christian love is sharply defined by an event: *"God sent his only Son into the world"* to give us life. It is love that issues in self-sacrificing, costly action to meet real need.

The term used to describe this love of God for us is *agape*. It was a rather nondescript, insignificant Greek word before it was transformd into one of the most beautiful, meaningful words of the language by its use in Christian circles. *Agape* came to mean self-giving love that knows absolutely no limits. The overriding, consuming desire of this kind of love is to seek the welfare of the person loved.

No sacrifice is so great, no suffering so painful, no ordeal so excruciating as to deter its commitment to the well-being of others.

The amazing characteristic of *agape* is that it is not conditioned by the response of the person loved. As the phrase in 1 John has it, *"not that we loved God."* God loves us when we do not love him—even when we are indifferent or hostile to the expressions of his love. Such love has to be prepared for the worst possible ignominy, the most painful of all experiences. It must be prepared to be rejected, refused, mocked, spit upon. In other words, it must be ready to go to a cross. That is exactly what happened in the case of Jesus. But even in the bleakness of that last hour there was never any alteration in the constancy of his love.

What does this mean for those who have become aware that God loves them? The conclusion drawn in verse 11 is indeed a surprising one. We would be prepared for him to say: "If God so loved us, we ought to love him in return." But he does not say that here.

Instead we read: *"If God so loved us, we also ought to love one another."*

To be sure, love for God is a response to be expected from the person who is aware of God's love for him. But we must remember that *agape* manifests its genuine character when it is directed toward people who are not easy to love. The only way that we show that the undeserved love of God flows through our lives is when we direct it toward other people like us.

We are very ingenious at thinking up excuses for not loving people. It is always easy to point to something that *they* did or said and use this as a justification for our hostility toward them. Sometimes our acceptance of people hinges on something so superficial as their not using a deodorant.

We must ever remember that *agape* is not tested by the people who are easy to love and who are good and kind to us. Any pagan can love somebody like that. It certainly does not require the grace of God to love sweet, lovable, generous people. Nor do we have to be Christians to reciprocate acts of kindness.

It is when the other person has said a harsh, critical word that he is difficult to love. I often tell my students that they need at least one church member who does not agree with them, nor compliment their sermons, nor support their plans for the church. Otherwise, they will never have an opportunity to show that they know what grace really means.

We are supposed to love other people solely and simply because *"God so loved us."* And we are neither lovable, good, or worthy. This robs us of all our excuses and rationalizations for not loving others. The fact that they are neither good nor responsive to our love is quite beside the point. Their slights, criticisms, difficult temperament only give us the occasion to exercise the kind of love we have received from God.

"No man has ever seen God." This is one of the real obstacles to faith in our modern, scientific, rationalistic world. The existence of God cannot be verified by the senses. The so-called proofs for the existence of God that seemed so convincing centuries ago do not have the same appeal to our contemporaries. Persons equally sincere and honorable can argue both for and against the existence of God on the basis of proofs from creation and nature.

But there is one genuine indication of the existence of

God in the world. Where brothers and sisters of the family of God love one another with the kind of love we have been talking about, there God becomes a vital presence in the world. Conversely, the absence of love makes all our talk about God meaningless and contradictory.

In my experience people who have known what it is to be loved genuinely find it easy to believe in God. On the other hand, people who have known only rejection and coldness find it extremely difficult to believe in God. Many of us can affirm that our darkest hours of doubt have come when we felt isolated by the hostility or indifference of others. The beginning of religious doubt is so often cynicism about the possibility of being able to trust the love of other people.

No doubt the reader has perceived by now that we do not find in 1 John the orderly development that is the result when a writer moves from one thought to another in logical sequence. The discussion in this little book is cyclical. The author returns again and again to the same themes, the most important of which we discussed in chapter one.

In verses 13 ff. we have a good example of the cyclical argument of 1 John. Christian assurance is based on our experience of the presence of God's Spirit in our lives. God's Spirit leads us to know that he sent his Son into the world. It also leads us to accept him as he comes to us in the Son. When we so accept him, God abides in us and gives us the assurance of his love. This leads us to verse 17 where an advance is made on previous thought.

In 2:28 the writer has already touched on the theme of the Christian's confidence as he faces the future. There it was *"confidence for the day of judgment."* This confidence is based on the assurance that we have nothing to fear from a God who loves us as a father loves his children.

The Christian's sense of security depends to a great extent on his theology—on how he conceives of God. My forebears of primitive Baptist stock worshiped an extremely stern and forbidding God. They majored on divine retribution and wrath. Their preaching was filled with thunder and lightning.

This concept of God was passed on to me early in life. As I remember it, this was the idea of God that was generally held by people in the church circles in which I was reared. I experienced some dark nights of terror in my early teens, when I wondered what tortures God had devised in his wrath for a boy who had not been very good the previous day.

Then I began to see that something important was missing in this picture of God. It did not take seriously what Jesus taught his followers about a heavenly Father who was far better and more compassionate than any human father could possibly be. The people of his day also had a distorted idea about God which he spent a lot of time attempting to correct. It is ironic that our concept of God frequently has more in common with the one that Jesus challenged than with the one that he communicated.

If we know that someone really loves us, it is impossible to be afraid of him. *"Perfect love casts out fear."* Insofar as we are afraid of God, our love is still immature or imperfect. Fear is a contradiction of love. It is inspired by the belief that God is against us. In his acceptance of and identification with outcasts and sinners, Jesus proclaimed the gospel of grace. God does not have the same attitude toward such people that society has. Grace means that God is for us.

The writer says: *"Fear has to do with punishment."* This

may be the correct translation of the meaning of the phrase.
Literally translated, however, the text reads: "Fear has punishment." This can mean that fear contains its own punishment within itself, that it is in effect its own punishment.
The fearful person suffers the tortures of the damned now,
whatever his fate in the future may be. It is not God's
purpose to produce fear but to elicit love. So the attitude of
the Christian should be one of loving confidence in God
from whom we have nothing to fear—now or forever.

God Is Our Brother's Father
1 John 4:19–5:5

We have learned that *agape* is the undeserved, unlimited,
self-sacrificing love of God expressed most vividly in the life
and death of Jesus. When people respond to this kind of
love, they in turn become the channels through which it
flows toward others. God's love, therefore, is prior to ours
and, in fact, is the source from which our love issues. This is
why the writer states: *"We love, because he first loved us."*

This does not mean that our love arises as a response to
his. In this case its source would still be from within us.
What it does mean is that the very possibility itself of our
loving in the way that God has loved us arises from the fact
that we possess a new life of love with which God has
endowed us. In other words, the capacity to love is itself a
gift of grace.

Our *agape* for others is the most characteristic expression
of the life that God gives us. If the love of God abides in us,
it cannot be fenced in; it is neither selfish nor prejudiced.
Love coming in from God will be going out to others,
because this is its very nature. Consequently, when this love
does not reach out from us to others, it says only one thing.

The origin of our life is not what we claim it to be. A life that is closed toward our brothers is a life that is also closed toward God. Therefore, *"if any one says, 'I love God,' and hates his brother, he is a liar."* Hate for our brothers is antithetical to and a contradiction of God's love.

It is clear that what we are talking about is not mere humanism. Loving man is not the same as loving God. From the Christian point of view, it is not possible to love man in the highest sense until we have the experience of first being loved by God. Many humanists have put professing Christians to shame by their concern and compassion for their fellow human beings and by their dedication to the welfare of others. But this does not mean that humanism contains the best answer to the tensions of a world torn apart by selfishness and ill-will. It does mean that multitudes of professing Christians are a living contradiction to the gospel.

Love for others is based properly on a genuine evaluation of their worth. The highest estimate of the value of a man is not found in humanism but in the biblical view of man. It begins with the concept that man is created in the image of God and stands at the apex of his creative work. It reaches its climax in the Christian conviction that all men are objects of God's ultimate, sacrificial love expressed in Jesus Christ. Our regard for others should be far higher, therefore, than that held by people who do not have this insight into the supreme worth of a human being.

First John poses the alternatives in human relations in stark, clearly defined alternatives. There is no middle ground. Either you *love* your brother or you *hate* him. This will strike many people as too radical and overdrawn.

Why can't I have the comfort of choosing a third option?

It ought to be quite enough that I just mind my own business and leave the other fellow alone. Or, that I don't wish anybody else any harm. Or, that I take a neutral position in the social tensions of our times. Multitudes of nice people take refuge in such attitudes and even mistakenly think of them as Christian. But we are not allowed to escape from the demands of God's love into bland neutrality.

First John classifies everything less than active, self-sacrificing dedication to the welfare of others as hatred. Neutrality toward our brothers is hatred. Indifference or neglect is also hatred. There are people who are guilty of exploiting others by paying them a substandard wage or by charging exorbitant prices for goods. One of the scandals of our society is that those people who can afford it less are often those who have to pay the highest rates of interest on money borrowed or goods purchased on installment. Children may not have enough to eat and wear or they may not have the chance for a good education because their parents are so exploited. Multitudes of other children do not have much of a chance in life because their parents are irresponsible or because they are abandoned by one or both of their parents. But am I less guilty if I have more than I need and fail to use it to meet such cases of human need?

God is not indifferent, negligent, or neutral toward anybody. Furthermore, believers in whose lives he has worked his miracle of grace cannot have these attitudes toward others. That is, insofar as their attitudes and acts express the reality of their relationship with God, they will be characterized by active commitment to seeking the welfare of others.

First John strips us of all the subterfuge that we use to

evade the meaning of the gospel in concrete human relations. He is not talking about love for others in some kind of general, abstract, sentimental attitude. Rather, he emphasizes that we must love the brother who is there—visible, concrete, disturbing: a mixture of good and bad, the possessor of attractive and unattractive traits.

I have heard many people remark in pious tones: "Oh, I know we should love their souls." By soul they seem to mean some invisible, intangible, abstract entity from which are missing all the qualities and characteristics that make it difficult to love people. A soul is presumably thought not to be black or white, rich or poor, educated or illiterate; neither is it conceived as dirty, diseased, or badly mannered. Little comfort can be found in the Bible for the idea that we can love the souls of people whose persons we refuse. In biblical terminology a person does not have a soul; he is a soul. This simply means that he is a living being.

The Christian is supposed to love people—the *"brother whom he has seen."* In the family of God there are brothers of all the colors of the human race, black and white, red and yellow. Some of them are refined; some are uncouth. Some of them are washed; others may not bathe once a week. Some use deodorant, some have never purchased any in their lives.

But God loves them all.

God does not love people in the abstract. He loves them as persons, with all their contradictions and all the traits that make it difficult to love them. When people open their lives to his love, they discover that it is a restless love, always reaching out to other human beings. The only way that we can really play it safe is to have nothing to do with

God's love. Then we can retain the privilege of deciding who is good enough for us to associate with.

In that way we can remain isolated in the ghetto of our indifference and take comfort in how religious we are and how much better than other people we are. It is dangerous for people to come into contact with God's love. It makes them do foolish, reckless, disturbing things. It makes them challenge the suffocating strictures of society that shut men off from one another. It causes them, thoughtless of their own security and position, to give themselves away in order to help others.

You see, the problem is that we do not choose our brothers and sisters in the family of God, just as we do not choose our blood brothers. I have one brother and one sister, neither of whom I requested. They were given to me by my parents without consultation with me. Just so does God present us with his other children, who become our brothers and sisters when we are brought into his family. We cannot claim him as Father, while at the same time we deny our relationship to them.

If we were permitted to choose other members of the family of God, we would probably make it a lot easier on ourselves to be Christian. We would select people who are easy to love. The family of our choice would be constituted of charming, gracious persons who possess the right social, educational, and family credentials.

But God has not surrendered to us the prerogative of setting the limits of his family. It is not constituted according to the categories of a prejudiced society. God gives to the Christian community only one option—that of accepting into their fellowship those whom God has accepted into his. If we are not prepared to make the circle of our love as broad as God's, we forfeit the right to belong to his family. How can we say that God lives in us if we frustrate his redemptive outreach to all men?

The statement in 1 John to this effect is disturbingly forthright: *"Every one who loves the parent loves the child."* No exceptions are opened, simply because the writer cannot conceive of a child of God who does not love the people whom God cares for so deeply.

Beginning with 5:2 we have another good example of the cyclical character of the argument in 1 John. Love for the children of God is closely bound up with God's love for us and our love for him. It is an expression of our love for God, which arises out of the life that he gives us. Again our love for God is not allowed to be dissipated into some kind of sentimental feeling, contemplation of the divine, or any such thing. Love for God makes us want to shape our lives by his will. For this has the love of God claimed us, for the highest and best fulfilment of our lives is to allow them to develop within the outline of his purpose, or, as the text expresses it, to *keep his commandments.* The central and crucial commandment, as we have already learned, is that we love one another.

Again, no exceptions.

Commandments has a forbidding, negative ring. In the minds of many people the connotation of commandments has to do with that which is negative, onerous, irksome, limiting, difficult to perform. The writer affirms, however, that God's commandments are not *burdensome* to his children.

Now I must admit that it is difficult for me to love other people, much more difficult than it is to preach about it or to write about it. It is more difficult for me to love others than it is to attend church, be a 100 percent in Sunday School, or live by an accepted moral code.

The truth of the matter is that God still has to love me more than I love other people and more than I deserve to be loved. The reason for this is that there are so many recalcitrant, rebellious areas of my life that have not been transformed by his love.

But God does not just command us to adopt a way of life that is difficult because it moves against the currents of our selfishness and bigotry. He comes into our lives to give us victory over the *world,* that is, over this selfish and rebellious spirit that opposes his purposes for our lives. He provides us with the resources that we need in order to live by his will. The energy of his love provides the power by which we live.

If we really believe that *"Jesus is the Son of God,"* not just with the tops of our heads but in the depth of our being, we are on the road to victory. Believing in Jesus involves commitment to a God who loves me. Believing in Jesus involves believing that God loves you. When I accept the God who comes to me in Jesus, I open my life to a tremendous liberating, conquering power that carries the promise of ultimate victory in all the dark, rebellious, nonloving areas of my life.

No, the commandment that we receive from him is not burdensome. Indeed, when his love is within us, it surges for expression. To have the opportunity to love others brings exultation to the life of God's child. God loves me more than I deserve to be loved. I can love him also, but never more than he deserves. I can never love him when he is hostile or indifferent to me.

My brother, however, is a different story. He is often

temperamental and harsh in his criticism. He disagrees with me. He isn't like me in so many ways. He cuts his hair differently, or doesn't cut it at all. He is different in appearance and dress, in taste and attitudes. There is one constant factor in all these brothers whom we see. They also need to be loved more than they deserve. I should be grateful to them when they are difficult to love, for only then can it really come through that God's grace has accomplished something in my life.

9

No Gospel Without the Cross

The gospel is the proclamation of God's great act of redemption in Jesus Christ. It is not the affirmation of abstract, theological ideas; its content is an event, a life, a tiny segment of the world's history. The Christian faith is based on the conviction that something happened in Palestine (a rather peripheral, small region of the Roman Empire) at a certain point in time (around the years A.D. 30–33) in the experiences of a man (Jesus of Nazareth) that has ultimate and crucial significance for the salvation of humanity.

For the Christian faith, therefore, the brief years of Jesus' ministry are the most important of all history. Little attention was given by the first followers of Jesus to his early life. Mark, our oldest written gospel, and John have nothing at all from this period. Matthew and Luke contain almost nothing beyond the birth narratives. No other book in the New Testament makes any reference at all to the life of Jesus before his actual ministry, apart from the affirmation that he was born a Jew of the seed of David.

Jesus' Decisive Years
I John 5:6–12

The decisive years were introduced with Jesus' baptism at the hands of John the Baptist and ended with his death on the cross. This was the period that had ultimate significance for salvation history. And of all the events of Jesus' life the passion is given the greatest prominence. Far more space is dedicated by our written gospels to those last days of Jesus' life than to any other comparable period. The closer we get to his death the more detailed are the accounts of the experiences of Jesus. There are reasons for this; early Christians had to explain why they worshiped a Lord who had been killed. At the same time, the emphasis on the death of Jesus shows how central it was.

It was exactly here that gnosticism threatened Christianity. From the gospel's central event, which consisted of the death and resurrection of Jesus Christ, it would have eliminated an indispensable part. We have already seen how this threatened the understanding of the gospel presented in 1 John. For the writer of our epistle the death of Jesus was the key to his concept of God as a God of infinite love, to his concept of the relation among believers as children of God, and to his interpretation of Christian ethics.

As we indicated in the introductory chapter, the teachers who rejected the gospel of early Christian history taught that the divine Christ had descended on Jesus at his baptism. This was their interpretation of the experience described in our written gospels at Mark 1:9–11; Luke 3:22; Matthew 3:13–17; and John 1:29–34.

The baptism, thus, seems to have figured very prominently in their teaching. But the cross was anathema to them. This is the problem with which the passage here under consideration comes to grips. The author argues in ways that he felt would be effective for his audience, but his reasoning is unusual and enigmatic for us. The basic message is nonetheless clear.

The *water* is a reference to the baptism of Jesus. The *blood* designates his crucifixion. The writer affirms that *Jesus Christ* (notice that the names identify the same person) was both baptized and crucified. *"The Spirit is the witness"* to the truth that the Jesus who was both baptized and crucified is the Son of God. This statement reminds us of the descent of the Spirit and the accompanying proclamation from heaven: "Thou art my beloved Son."

The writer may also be thinking of this. But he also believes that the Spirit is God's continuing and contemporary witness to the incarnation, leading people to confess Jesus as the Christ the Son of God. The event that was proclaimed by the early church continues to be authenticated in the life of the contemporary church by God through his Spirit.

In Jewish legal practice the testimony of a witness had to be corroborated by that of another in order to be accepted as evidence in court (Deut. 19:15). This furnishes the background for the argument used by 1 John. There are not two but three witnesses to the reality of the incarnation. These witnesses, the historical events of the baptism, and the crucifixion with the continuing testimony of the Spirit bear God's own witness as to whom Jesus really was.

The writer could not understand how people who would accept the corroborating testimony of two or more human witnesses could reject the evidence that God himself had given about his Son. The rejection of the evidence that God's own Son had actually died on the cross is construed as a rejection of the word of God himself. The people who taught that God's Son was not a genuine human being named Jesus were in effect making a *liar* out of God.

Through the centuries theologians have struggled to express the meaning of the death of Jesus in the language and thought patterns of their times. Some of these theories of the atonement seem even crude to us today. No one theory has ever done more than to help us catch a glimpse of one facet of the truth that shines from so many planes of this profoundly significant event. There are heights in it that the human spirit cannot scale, depths that the human mind cannot plumb, a breadth that the human imagination cannot comprehend. The sublime mystery of a God who undeservedly suffers himself in order to redeem men who deserve to suffer defies all explanation. The problem is that our western mind influenced by rationalism struggles to reduce our relationship with God to a logical, easily memorized, and repeated formula. This is impossible.

It remains true in the twentieth century, however, that our grasp of the truth that God is for us and that he loves us without limit is bound up with the death of Jesus. It is also true that our insights into what it means to be genuinely Christian also depend on the same event. Although the arguments and the language used in 1 John may seem at times to be somewhat strange to us, what it is talking about is still very much at the center of the Christian faith.

Just as it was in the first generations of Christian history, so does it remain today. The gospel is not the gospel unless it revolves around the proclamation that Christ died for us. Not to keep us from dying, to be sure, but to enable us to die and to be resurrected to live for God in a new life of love in fellowship with his children.

Before leaving this passage we shall take note of an interesting variation between the text of the Authorized or King James Version and that of more modern translations. Read the Authorized Version's words after 5:6.

These words are not found in any of the good manu-
scripts containing the text of 1 John, which indicates that
they were not a part of the original text. Consequently, they
are not important to an interpretation of the epistle. But
their presence in the King James Version is explained by an
unusual story that students of the New Testament will find
interesting.

It so happens that Erasmus, who edited the first pub-
lished printed Greek text of our New Testament, omitted
the passage in question because he did not find a single
Greek manuscript that contained it. However, it was in the
Vulgate, the Latin translation of the Bible then in general
use. Since the Vulgate was so highly esteemed, Erasmus was
criticized for having omitted a part of the Word of God. In
just the same way other scholars have been harshly judged
for daring to tamper with the accepted texts in an effort to
bring them closer to the original.

As a reaction to this criticism made by a leading scholar
named Stunica, Erasmus promised to include the disputed
words in a subsequent edition if he found one Greek manuscript to support such a text. In due course such a manuscript was produced, probably representing a translation
from the Vulgate into the Greek. It was made by someone
who would not allow ethics to deter him from his efforts to
restore the "Word of God." True to his promise, Erasmus
included the passage in his third edition. This became the
basis for the accepted text in England that was used subse-
quently by the translators of the KJV.

10

Blessed Assurance

It is sometimes unjustifiably assumed that a person who is a genuine Christian will never be troubled by doubts. Perhaps we who preach and teach have contributed to this false notion by intimidating people with our sermons on faith and Christian assurance.

Because we can talk about faith so glibly, our listeners may get the idea that we never experience the agony of uncertainty and doubt. I, for one, shall have to confess that it is much easier for me to talk about trust than it is to exercise it. I suspect that the same may be true for many other people. So the problem of doubt is compounded by the added agony of loneliness. The doubting person believes that if he were as dedicated as his fellow Christians he would have the assurance that they seem to have. So he dare not confess to them his weaknesses. It is really a vicious circle. By hiding our problems we give a hypocritical impression. Thus, we are prevented from confessing our weaknesses to one another and finding strength from one another in the fellowship of confession and prayer.

The Purpose of 1 John
1 John 5:13–15

If it were not possible for Christians to be thrown off balance by questions and doubts, 1 John would never have

111

been written. Nor, for that matter, would much of the rest of the New Testament have been written. It is exactly because Christians are troubled by unbelief that the author took the time to pen the lines that we have been studying.

We must recognize that 1 John was written specifically to Christians. The writer so states in 5:13, where he identifies his intended readers as persons *"who believe in the name of the Son of God."* If you are reading the King James Version, you notice that there is an additional clause: "And that ye may believe on the name of the Son of God." That clause is omitted from the later versions because it is not supported by the manuscript evidence. It was not a part of the original text of 1 John. The epistle was written solely to persons who believed that God's Son was the man Jesus.

These believers had been under pressure from teachers who questioned the validity of their faith and sought to undermine the basis of their religious experience. The purpose of the writer is to bring support to his fellow believers. He expresses his purpose in these words: *"That you may know that you have eternal life."*

Believers may experience dark hours of spiritual distress when they wonder if there is any substance at all in what they believe. Frequently, this results from contact with other persons who, like the teachers opposed in 1 John, raise questions about the foundations of the Christian faith. Is there really a God? How can we believe that there is any future for the individual beyond this life? In the midst of the cruel contradictions and inconsistencies of life, how can one believe in a God of love? Why should we believe that Jesus is any more unique for man's knowledge of God than Buddha, Confucius, or any other great religious genius?

No longer can believers live in isolation from the world

around them. They cannot build a wall high enough to keep ideas hostile to their faith from penetrating their community. It seems to me that we should not want to do so if we could. Blind, or ignorant, or provincial faith cannot be mature. The Christian is now forced to be aware of the environment in which he is to live out his faith. All kinds of doubts, religious cynicism, questions, and conflicting ideas are piped into our homes through our television sets.

To be sure, we must understand that our faith needs correcting, that our knowledge of evidence is incomplete, and that some of our ideas are erroneous. What we believe about God, the Bible, various theories of the atonement, and the like should always be open to new insights and be corrected by new knowledge.

But I am talking about those convictions that constitute the basis of the Christian faith. Whether we believe in God at all, whether we believe he loves us, whether we believe in the uniqueness of his revelation of Jesus Christ, whether we believe in the future—these are the matters that relate to the very center of our faith.

We have been talking to this point about doubts raised through contact with persons and ideas who challenge our faith. But sometimes our doubts arise out of our own experiences. In moments of loneliness, disillusion, and despair God can seem awfully far away and unreachable. We may get the idea that this whole business of belief in God is just a cruel hoax.

Yes, Christians may have experiences like this. Even good Christians often do. But we cannot say that this is the ideal for the Christian life. The goal of Christian faith is complete trust in a good and capable Father which will allay the anxieties and insecurities that we experience from life in the world. Perfect *confidence* in God brings the conviction that we can go to him with our needs and that he will provide for us.

The Bible does not view prayer as a kind of magic abracadabra by which we control God. We can never put God into a corner and force his hand by anything that we do. His providential care is always a free, undeserved gift —never the result of anything we do. However we may interpret it, therefore, prayer is not the imposition of our will on God.

It is an expression of our trust in him and of our total dependence upon him for life and for the resources necessary to meet its problems and opportunities. The prayer of the child who trusts his heavenly Father is made *according to his will*. Always and in every circumstance we can trust the will of a Father who wants only the highest and best for his child.

When what we ask of our Father is in accord with his purpose for our lives, *he hears us*. In biblical terminology for God to hear us means that he finds our prayer to be acceptable. He receives it. We can be confident that the God who thus hears will also answer our prayers.

I had a missionary colleague in Brazil who possessed what we often hear referred to as "simple, childlike" faith. Whenever a problem or a need arose, he talked to God about it. After he had prayed about the matter, he never worried about it again, insofar as I could tell. He had turned his needs over to God and was confident that whatever God did about the problem would be exactly right. This is the kind of security that Jesus talks about in the Sermon on the Mount (Matt. 6:25 ff.). The possession of it and the peace that flows from it is a genuine possibility in the Christian experience. It is a shame that so few of us ever come close to attaining it.

Assurance in Prayer for the Erring Brother
1 John 5:16–17

The writer has asserted confidently that God hears and answers the prayers of his children. So far, so good. Most of us who are Christians find nothing to quarrel with there. But when he gives a specific illustration of this principle, he creates quite a problem for some of us. God forgives our *brother* his sins when we pray for him!

Let us understand first of all that 1 John is talking about prayer for fellow Christians. *Brother* is used where we use the term Christian or church member. The writer does not speak at all about the significance of prayer by Christians for people who do not profess faith.

The writer's illustration creates difficulties for those of us who belong to groups that stress the responsibility of each individual to seek forgiveness for his own sins. By the same token, it is easily interpreted as a biblical justification for the specialized role of the priest who hears the confession of the penitent and offers up prayers for his forgiveness.

Much of the conflict between religious groups has occurred because they tend to emphasize one truth to the exclusion of the other. Often what we need to do is to hold to both truths and try to understand how they relate to one another.

The New Testament definitely teaches that forgiveness is granted to the person who is open to it. No one stands between any individual and God as a "necessary" mediator. God is just as accessible to you and just as willing to receive you as any other of his children. The prayer of priest or of pastor has no more influence with God than that of the least of his children.

Nevertheless, the New Testament also teaches that Christians as individuals and as a community are responsible for the believer who has a moral problem. This responsibility is set forth by Paul in Galatians 6:1–2: "Brethren, if a man is overtaken in any trespass, you who are spiritual should restore him in a spirit of gentleness. Look to yourself, lest you too be tempted. Bear one another's burdens, and so fulfil the law of Christ."

True enough, this is not a responsibility that is delegated to one group in the church alone. Every Christian is a priest in the sense that he can be a channel through whom a person finds God and through whom God's grace becomes effective and real in another's life.

So the New Testament teaches both that an individual is responsible before God for his own life and that he also has a role to play in the forgiveness of his brother. The problem is to understand how these two relate to one another in a meaningful way.

Before we go any further, we must talk about this enigmatic phrase *mortal sin*. This concept in certain religious circles is used to describe particularly grave sins, such as murder and adultery. The person who commits this kind of sin and dies without confessing it or without the intention to confess it is consigned to eternal punishment, according to the theological view of some.

Admittedly, the writer of 1 John might have defined mortal sin in any number of ways in his own mind. But he does not explain here exactly what he has in view. The only clue is that the persons who may commit such sins are also *brothers,* or members of the churches.

The only safe approach to interpretation is to attempt to understand a passage in the context of the total book or group of books written by an author. Our author refers to only one group of church members whom he considers to be outside the pale of Christian fellowship. They are the false teachers who deny the reality of the incarnation, whom he also describes as antichrists. They either were or had been participants in the congregations (cf. 2:19). There was always the possibility that their number would grow as other members adhered to their teaching.

We are probably right in believing, therefore, that the denial of the incarnation is the mortal sin or, literally, "sin unto death," mentioned in 1 John. The writer does not recommend prayer for those people who were guilty of it. They had denied that God has come to them in love in Jesus Christ. They had denied the validity of his life as the moral tension under which Christians live. Consequently, they could neither understand their need for forgiveness nor what forgiveness really meant.

It would be wrong for us to suppose on the basis of this passage that any person is ever hopelessly lost. No one ever lives so wickedly or sins so desperately that God ceases to love him or to offer him the possibility of reconciliation. If the cross means anything at all, it means this. Too many people on the basis of bad theology and poor preaching and teaching have concluded that they are irrevocably and eternally lost. They believe that they have committed a sin that cuts them off from God forever. This passage does not justify such an idea at all. There is nothing at all to keep us from believing that anybody, no matter what his previous situation is, will be accepted by God if he turns to him in repentance.

The sins of fellow Christians for which our writer recommends prayer are those moral lapses which occur in all our lives. They may include such things as gossiping, ill-will toward others, anger toward a brother, drunkenness, lying, and many other kinds of immorality. We are assured that our brother will be given *life,* that is, he will be forgiven, if we pray for him.

In the circles that I have known we generally deal with the brother in one of two ways, both of which are wrong. Sometimes, we isolate him from the Christian community. If we do not actually exclude him from the church (and this is not practiced much any more), we isolate ourselves from him by our condemning, harsh attitudes. We let him know that we do not want to have anything to do with him unless he gets his life straightened up. If he will give up his wrongdoing, ask God's forgiveness, and let us know that he is changed, then we are willing to take him back into our fellowship.

Generally, however, we deal with our erring brother in the opposite fashion. We simply ignore his problem. We talk to him about the weather, sports, politics, and a hundred other subjects, all the while pretending that we do not know that he has a spiritual difficulty. If we say anything about it at all, we say it to someone else and not to him.

In either case the weak brother is left to struggle with his failures and guilt alone. The Christian community fails him just when his need is the greatest and then usually commits the further sin of reproaching him because he did not have the strength to cope with his problems without the support of others.

We are supposed to pray for our needy brother. This

does not mean for us to go into our closet to pray in isolation from him. It means rather that we are to offer to him the support of our prayers in time of need. We are to bring him into the fellowship of the community and ask God's forgiveness for him. All this presupposes that he is our brother and that he will respond to our ministry to him.

Naturally, we must minister to him in great humility. Even as I pray for my brother who has sinned, I am aware that tomorrow I will need this ministry from him. We cannot live the Christian life in isolation from our brothers. The loneliness of sin and guilt is an anguish too great for us to bear. If other Christians are indifferent to me or treat me with spiritual arrogance, it deepens the problem of my guilt. It gives me the idea that they are not sinners like me, else they would be willing to share the burden of my sin. It is this sense of inadequacy, this feeling that we are morally and spiritually inferior to others, which afflicts so many Christians and denies to them the peace that is produced when the grace of God is made real in the Christian community.

I have a friend who is an alcoholic. For many years he attended church services regularly and supported Christian causes financially but was not otherwise active in the life of the church. Everybody knew that he was an alcoholic. This was an effective barrier against his giving a convincing testimony to his faith. Who is going to listen to a person like that?

In the course of time he had an unusual religious experience and, as a result, was able to quit drinking. Then he was able to do all the things that he had always wanted to do. He became a deacon in the church, a Sunday School teacher, and an extremely effective Christian witness in the community. After a few years of real involvement in the life of the church, he went through a period of great stress in which more was thrown on him than he was able to bear. As a result, he began to drink again.

Do you know what the church did? Nothing. Nothing at all. Everybody remarked that Jim had gone back to drinking again. This was really not surprising to the people who had known him before. But nobody went to him to make an attempt to bring him back into the fellowship of the community. Nobody said to him: "For ten years you have been a source of strength and inspiration to me. Now I want to stand by you. I simply am not going to let you go. I want to bear this burden with you."

The last that I knew of Jim, he was bearing his guilt in the loneliness that he had known for so many years. He feels cut off from God and suffers from a great sense of inadequacy and inferiority. He is sure that those other Christians, who seem from his point of view to be so sure of themselves and so impervious to weaknesses, must be immensely superior to him. He really feels that they are closer to God than he is. The truth of the matter is that they are not, of course. If they had been close to God, they would have been impelled to reach out to their brother in need.

In the rugged individualism that has determined so much of our theology, we have missed out on the meaning and role of the believing community. If we ever perceive what tremendous power there is in a community of people who know what it means to be under the grace of God, we shall really begin to see the lame walk, the blind see, and the deaf hear. In the meantime, we just go around telling people that they ought to be good and wonder why more of them are not.

Assurance Expressed in Christian Certainties
1 John 5:18–21

As long as the believer focuses his attention on himself, he will be plagued by doubts and insecurity. There is so much that we cannot know; there is so much that we cannot do. But Christian assurance is not based on our own moral resources or theological sophistication. It is properly based on convictions about God and his love and power.

This is where our writer begins in the first of three great affirmations of victorious assurance: *"We know that any one born of God does not sin, but He who was born of God keeps him."* The substance of this affirmation is that the One who keeps the Christian possesses greater power than the *evil one*. For this reason, the one who is *born of God does not sin*.

We have already seen in our discussion of 2:29–3:10 that statements like this cannot mean that the believer never commits acts of sin. This would be contradicted very clearly by the verses just above (5:16–17) where the writer talks about the need for prayer on behalf of the sinning brother. What these statements do mean is that the believer "does not keep on sinning" (present tense). Evil is not the power that dominates the life of the Christian. His life belongs to God, and he is kept by the power of God's Son. Therefore, *"the evil one does not touch him,"* in the sense that he is not a captive or slave to the power of evil. The evil one does not determine his life nor his destiny.

But what we believe about God's greatness and power does not in itself bring assurance. We must have the personal assurance that we belong to this God whose power is greater than the power of evil. In the second place, there-

fore, the writer expresses the conviction that he and the
Christians whom he addresses *are of God*. In other words,
they are begotten of God and, consequently, are assured
that they have moved from the world of rebellion, sin, and
death into the relationship with God that is life. From the
point of view taken in 1 John, a person is either under
God's power or under the *power of the evil one*. If he
belongs to the family of God, he can live a life of confidence
even in the midst of the corruption and sin of the surround-
ing world.

But there are gods many and lords many. When the
believer is asked: "To which God do you belong?" there is
only one answer. He is the God who has come to me in
Jesus Christ. He is the God and Father of our Lord Jesus
Christ. All this goes back to a certain point in time, to a
certain place in the world, and to a certain Man—Jesus of
Nazareth, who was crucified under Pontius Pilate. *"And we
know that the Son of God has come and has given us
understanding, to know him who is true."*

As we said in the beginning, this does not mean that God
is a prisoner to the past, no matter how glorious and meaningful the past may have been. God must come to me today
in my own experience and in my own life. Believing facts
about God is no substitute for a personal experience of
God.

But how am I to identify this God in the welter of
religious ideas of our world? I always identify him with
reference to Jesus of Nazareth. My interpretation of my
experience of God is indissolubly linked with my understanding of the life, death, and resurrection of Jesus Christ.
This is the *true God,* the possessor and source of *eternal
life.*

When we say this, we do not have to believe that God is not present in other religious cultures or that he has not been active in other places in history and in his world. Neither does our belief that the one true God has revealed himself in Jesus of Nazareth equip us to determine the destiny of people who do not know the Christian gospel.

People inquire frequently about my opinion concerning persons who never heard the gospel. Are they lost or saved? If you have in mind the ultimate destiny of such people, I will have to reply: "I am not equipped to answer your question. I can neither judge nor save people. That is God's prerogative and God's alone." You may want to quote Scripture to me. But I must still contend that even with the Bible you are not God.

I believe, however, that the person who does not hear or accept the gospel is lost in the sense that he cannot know the genuine meaning of life. Whatever may be his lot beyond death, his experience in life has been much poorer and more limited than it might have been.

If we believe that God created us and that he has claimed us by his love in Jesus Christ, we must believe that the chief end of existence is to love and serve him forever. Anything short of this is idolatry.

It may seem strange that believers who know the Father of Jesus Christ, the one true God, would have to be warned against idolatry. But idol worship is an ever-present danger.

The worship of anything less than God is idolatry. What we worship is what we serve, which may be different from what we sing and talk about. Bad things can be idols, but good things can also be idols. Idols may be money or property, pleasure or self. But even religion and church become idols when they stand in the way of our living for God.

Religion is idolatrous when it makes us self-righteous, unfeeling, and harsh. Church is an idol when it gets us involved in a lot of activities that keep us from serving God. In fact, it can be a very dangerous idol, because when we are busy with religious programs we may get the idea that we are serving God. Culture and country can be idols if they, instead of God, determine our moral standards and style of life.

We need to recognize that idolatry is very pervasive and often difficult to define. We need the warning with which 1 John ends, therefore, just as much as do people who worship crude images of clay or stone: *"Little children, keep yourselves from idols."*

For
Further
Reading

Because of the relevance of First John to the contemporary life, you may be interested in other reading of a contemporary nature. The publisher would recommend the following book.

John's Letters—Light for Living by Landrum P. Leavell. (Nashville: Broadman Press, 1970, 96 pages.) Here is practical and inspirational help in understanding and teaching the letters of John.